HUBBLE STITCH 2
Further adventures into planet Hubble

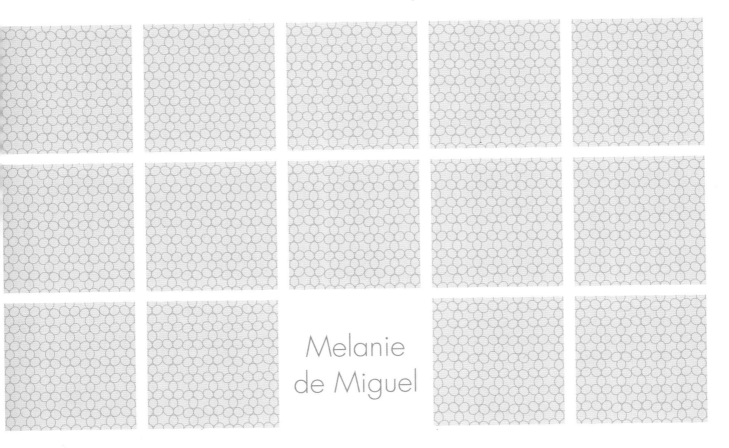

Melanie
de Miguel

Hubble Stitch 2 Further adventures into planet Hubble © Melanie de Miguel
ISBN 978-1-909116-72-6

Published in 2016 by SRA Books

SRA Books
www.suerichardson.co.uk

The right of Melanie de Miguel to be identified as the author of this work has been asserted by her in accordance with the Copyright, Designs and Patents Act 1988.

A CIP record of this book is available from the British Library.

Photography © Michael Wicks
www.michaelwicks.com

Melanie wishes to encourage you to explore the new Hubble stitch and create your own patterns and projects using it. If you develop work based on the ideas or projects in this book, she would be grateful if you would credit her as designer. This would also be appreciated if you use the ideas to submit pieces to magazines or books or to teach in a professional capacity.

There is a Facebook group for Hubble Stitch where you are welcome to submit your pictures and share your ideas and projects with Melanie and your fellow Hubblers.
www.facebook.com/HubbleStitch

Finally, if you do find any errors or you have any questions, please contact us as we would be delighted to have the opportunity to make corrections in the next print run.

Printed and bound in the United Kingdom.

FOREWORD BY MARCIA DECOSTER

Brilliant! That's the word that first came to mind after reading *Hubble Stitch 2* from cover to cover in one sitting. I quickly jotted down a message to Melanie with that one word, promising a few more words to describe her latest book.

Besides brilliant, the first thing I noticed was how conversational the book's text was. Melanie's vibrant personality is evident on every page and the conversational style of the book makes it easy to read and understand. Her enthusiasm and passion for the science of the stitch is infectious. Melanie's newest exploration into Hubble stitch brings us the Wave Hubble – an even slinkier and more fabric-like stitch then the original Hubble she introduced us to in *Let's Hubble!*.

She starts out by giving us a 'language' for Hubble, including the terms 'Wave Hubble', 'snuggle up' (the perfect description for aligning the adjacent units), 'cast on', which creates the foundation row and 'inverted Hubbles' referring to the upside down Hubble stitch which creates the wave pattern.

Chapter One explains the basic concept of the Wave Hubble and presents the beautiful Metamorphose cuff to get us started. Graphics and text lead us through learning the stitch and give us row-by-row instruction for completing the first project. In each of the chapters there is also a section suggesting variations to help us imagine other possibilities.

Through the choice of projects that are unveiled, a chapter at a time, we get to see the breadth of possibility this technique affords us. Beyond the first beautiful cuff, we see Wave Hubble used to create patterns with helpful charts to get us started on our own patterning.

Each chapter builds on the skill sets needed to be successful with Wave Hubble and increases our confidence, while making a wide variety of wearable jewelry. We are treated to earrings, bracelets and necklaces as well as techniques we can later use to bezel or create ropes, toggles and toroids. There's also a gallery of pieces made with the techniques described in that chapter. The last chapter brings us a project that incorporates all of the learning we've done throughout the book and results in the beautiful sand dollars bracelet, which sets rivolis into the Wave Hubble toroid presented earlier in the chapter.

Her workshop tips help to re-enforce and clarify some of the more complicated concepts and keep us steadily improving our Wave Hubble knowledge. Melanie easily shares her knowledge as she has delved deeply into the stitch's capabilities and knows just where to add an extra few words to help us along.

While learning a new stitch can sometimes be intense, the approach is so well thought out and presented that there is an easy path to getting comfortable and proficient in creating not only the projects presented but those you might envision. There's a liberal dose of humour along with Melanie-isms such as 'Right, that's enough rhubarb, let's have a go...'

I firmly embraced the techniques in Melanie's first book *Let's Hubble!* and expect to do the same with this second in a series of her explorations into this wonderfully versatile stitch. I'm quite confident that with the body of knowledge Melanie shares in *Hubble Stitch 2* you'll want to do the same!

CONTENTS

INTRODUCTION

...

Hubble Stitch 2
Further adventures into
planet Hubble created by
Melanie de Miguel

INTRODUCTION

It's now been three years since I first experimented with the threadpath I came to know as Hubble stitch, and in that time I truly feel I've been on an incredible journey. Every single time I got out my beads, I found myself working in Hubble stitch and discovering new and more exciting ways of working it. If you're reading this, then you've probably come on that journey too and you are probably an avid Hubbler like me.

You may also have noticed that there's a bit of a spacey-scientific theme going on, unsurprisingly, given the name Hubble. But I'm so glad I chose it because it's been the source of a lot of fun whilst teaching Hubble stitch. There are all the alliterations I started off – happy, Hooray Henry Hubbles, headstands etc., but my students in the initial stages have also been heard to utter some great ones – helpless, hapless, homeless, hearty, half-baked and even hungover Hubbles! When it comes to the scientific angle though, there's a lot to come – and we're talking physics. But don't get disheartened, it's just me playing with names!

By now you will have worked through the techniques in the first book – *Let's Hubble!* – so you'll have a good grounding in basic, 2-Drop, 3-Drop, circular and tubular, HorSO, VerSO and inverted Hubble. All of that was actually a prelude to this next technique, which I hope is as exciting for you as it was for me, because it blew my socks off! It's called Wave Hubble. You may remember in the first book I told you about the exciting variations that can happen because of that wonderful property of Hubble stitch – the fact that when you are working the foundation row, the individual stitches can swivel and turn independently of one another; well those Henrys doing headstands play a big part in Wave Hubble. I discovered Wave Hubble whilst on holiday in summer 2014, and, at the time, I was seriously contemplating writing the first book when I produced a little swatch of Basic Wave Hubble. This was another one of those sit up and gasp moments and I then made swatches in 2-Drop and 3-Drop; I was so astonished that I knew I had to crack on and write that book to share Hubble stitch with the beading world because, unless I did, I wouldn't be able to tell anyone about Wave Hubble!

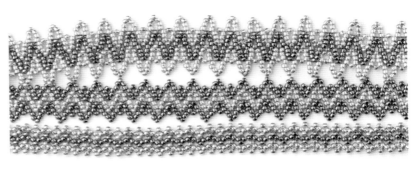

Once again, in planning and writing this book, I have tried to set out a logical pathway of discovery and learning for you, as I did in *Let's Hubble!*, with workshop tips throughout, to help with reality checks and troubleshooting issues that can arise. I want to take you by the hand and guide you, step by step, through some amazing places on planet Hubble!

The initial chapters introduce you to Wave Hubble and all its astonishing, technical variations, including Basic, Picture and Interference Wave Hubble, plus of course, 2-Drop and 3-Drop Wave and the HorSO versions. You will also learn how to blend Basic, 2-Drop and 3-Drop, seamlessly one into the other, to create an awesome fan effect.

You may remember the idea of building bracelets or cuffs vertically or horizontally. Those built vertically grow in length to reach around your wrist, whilst those built horizontally grow in width, which means the foundation row has to be the length of the bracelet. I applied that same horizontal concept to making Wave Hubble ropes which involved a really satisfying zipping up process! You'll experience just how fine and slinky these ropes can be and then later, in the last chapter, we'll have some fun with the rope concept, creating toroid shapes and toggles.

If you thought Hubble stitch created great, flexible textiles like material, then you'll find those produced by Wave Hubble have an even more amazing, lacy slinkiness to them. I just love holding them up to the light to see the beautiful patterns they make.

My comments about materials and tools in the first book still stand. I really enjoy working with Miyuki seed beads because of their even quality, and Fireline (4lb) because of its beautiful 'slidey' property which is always a big help when snuggling! There are a couple of updates in Notes and Terms below, in particular there are going to be changes as to how you snuggle up when working Wave Hubble, but all will be revealed in Chapter 1.

As before, size 12 needles will be fine to use for learning the techniques and working all the projects in this book, but you will need to use size 13-14 needles if you start working with size 15° Czech Charlottes, particularly when securing the clasps.

Right! Beads, needles and thread at the ready? Let's go!

Notes, Terms and Abbreviations

To work any of the instructions and projects in this book, it's helpful to familiarise yourself with the terms I use:

Wingspan	The length of thread to be used; holding the end of the thread in one hand and the reel in the other just spread your arms wide apart like wings, and cut that length.
Snuggle up	This is my way of describing the action of sliding beads or stitches up close to each other to make them touch, leaving no thread visible between them. Ordinary Hubbles must still only just touch, whereas Wave Hubbles must be locked together closely.
Tail thread	Unless specified otherwise, always leave a tail thread of approximately 15cm/6"; this is an optimum length both for gripping your beadwork and for ease of sewing in at the end.
Finish off	Weave back through your work, making a few half hitch knots along the way, and cut the thread where it emerges.
Work in	Join in a new thread thus: insert the needle into the beadwork a short distance away from the point where you wish to begin beading again; weave through to where you want to emerge, following the previous thread paths, and making a few half hitch knots on the way, then cut off the tail end of the new thread.
Best location for half hitch knots	I found that the best place to make those knots when working in and finishing off thread is between 2 Hubble stitches, where their arm beads touch, as the knot will be totally hidden in the tight joint.
Tension	It is very important that you always maintain a good, even tension when working in any form of Hubble.

Cast on	This term refers to making the foundation stitches, for example, cast on 10 Hubble stitches means work a foundation row of 10 Hubble stitches.
Close the row and secure it	When working a circular/tubular row you will always have to join the last stitch onto the 1st, which closes the row. For Hubble stitch this always means passing up into the presenting, outer arm bead (or beads) of the 1st stitch, and on through the head bead. Generally the join will have to be secured by passing around all beads of the 1st stitch, emerging from the head in the stepped up position, ready to start the new row.
WH	Wave Hubble is spoken about so much in this book that it's easiest to abbreviate to the initials. There's also another form called Interference Wave Hubble, which becomes IWH.
'Pick up' abbreviations	For projects throughout the book there will be a need for a shorthand method of indicating which colour beads need to be picked up. Foundation row stitches always require 2 arm beads and 1 body bead for Phase 1, then a head bead for Phase 2, so the abbreviation for the pick-up sequence would be, for example, 2A,1B+1A or 1A,1B,1C+1A, etc. From the 2nd row onwards, upright basic Hubbles require 2 arm beads only in Phase 1, and 1 head bead in Phase 2, so I have abbreviated this to, for example, 2A+1A or 2B+1A or 1A,1B+1B, etc. Inverted Basic Hubbles are more straightforward as they simply require 3 beads to be picked up, which may or may not be all the same colour, for example, 3A or 2A,1B or 1B,2A, etc.
Reading grids and diagrams	I have drawn grids and diagrams to be read from the bottom upwards, with the newest rows in diagrams added to the top. Read L-R for odd rows (1, 3, 5, 7, etc.), and R-L for even rows (2, 4, 6, 8, etc.).

CHAPTER ONE

· · ·

Basic Wave Hubble

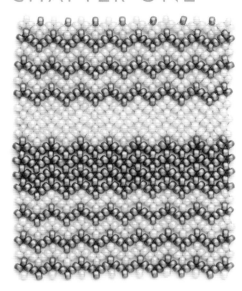

Basic Wave Hubble

Remember how fiddly that foundation Hubble row can be, especially when you first tried it out; how those rather naughty Henry Hubbles want to do their own thing and swivel? And what about how you also had to work on your tension to get their arms just to touch? Well, you're gonna love this. These Hubbles are snuggled up to the max and they're arranged in a one-up, one-down formation. Your foundation row will be a great deal easier to handle.

I've found the simplest way to learn WH is to use 2 contrasting colours (A and B), as they will help you to see clearly which Hubble is up and which is down, just until you get used to the formation and then you can do your own thing colour-wise. Each stitch will be worked using a main colour for the arms and head beads and a contrast colour for the body bead. Switch the colours around to alternate rows and this really shows up the waves. Work little swatches using about 1m/40" thread, in a bead size that is comfortable for you.

Foundation Row:

1. **Phase 1**: Make one basic Hubble thus: pick up 2A,1B and make the body ring by passing the needle again through the first A bead picked up, in the same direction.

Tail thread

Working thread

2. **Phase 2**: Pick up 1A for the head and pass the needle through the adjacent A bead of the ring.

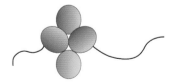

3 Work a 2nd basic Hubble exactly as before.

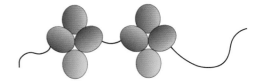

4 Now snuggle them up so that the 2nd Hubble actually flips upside down, and its arm slides under the arm of the first Hubble. There should be no thread showing at all between them.

5 Work a 3rd Hubble and snuggle it up tightly as before.

6 Continue working basic Hubbles and really snuggling them up, so that they are arranged in the up-down formation. Finish with an odd number of stitches.

Workshop Tip 1: I would work a foundation row of 9 stitches for your practice swatch (or any other odd number). The reason for doing an odd number is that when you step up, it will allow you to work the first stitch as normal. I'll explain all shortly. Once you get the hang of WH you'll be able to work it from an even number of stitches too. But let's walk before we run!

Workshop Tip 2: Here you can see a real foundation row of WH. Normally the stitches will stay in their up-down formation but occasionally as you continue to work and manipulate the beadwork, some may flip over. This is not a problem because you'll be able to put them right when working the 2nd row, so you don't need to fiddle around with them to try and line them up nicely before you continue.

7️⃣ Step up as normal (with the thread currently emerging from the arm bead, continue on through the body bead, other arm bead and head bead, as in the diagram).

2nd Row: Now we switch colours, so B is the main colour of the row, with A for the body beads.

8️⃣ 1st stitch – **Phase 1**: Pick up 2B and make the body ring by passing through the head bead of the foundation Hubble below.

9️⃣ (Still in **Phase 1**): Continue on through the first of the 2 beads just picked up, and snuggle up.

10 **Phase 2**: Pick up 1B and position the head as normal.

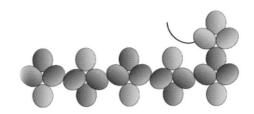

Workshop Tip 3: Here's where it all changes. The next stitch of the foundation row is inverted (you can clearly see the differently coloured body bead presenting itself, and if it's not behaving, then turn it to copy the inverted Hubble in the step 10 diagram), so the stitch you are about to make on top of it, must also be inverted. As you would with the 2nd row of normal Hubble stitch, you still need to be somewhat vigilant that the foundation stitches are correctly orientated, but once you get to the 3rd row, they are set in their positions as usual.

Workshop Tip 4: Remember, for inverted Hubble stitch you need to pick up and make the entire base of 3 beads (as if making a foundation stitch) before passing through the head bead in the **forward** direction (not a backstitch because, for inverted Hubble, everything is topsy-turvy). Right, that's enough rhubarb, let's have a go...

11 2nd stitch – **Phase 1**: Pick up 2B,1A, slide the beads down close to the beadwork and pass once again through the 1st B bead picked up in the same direction. Don't worry about snuggling yet.

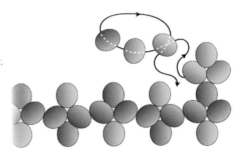

12 **Phase 2**: Check to ensure that the next stitch on the foundation row is inverted and pass forward through the presenting body bead.

If you stop to think about it, this is the same as picking up the head bead for a foundation stitch.

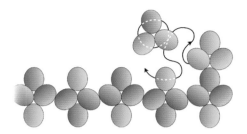

Workshop Tip 5: When you pass through the presenting body bead and start to draw the thread through to take up the slack, the little ring of 3 beads can twizzle around sometimes, leaving you unsure as to which bead is which. To ensure those beads are orientated correctly, use the tip of your needle as a guide to un-twizzle them, by sliding it into the gap as in the image, and pressing it against the ring.

13 **Phase 2** (cont.): Complete the stitch by passing through the arm bead, just as you would for a normal basic Hubble stitch after picking up the head bead.

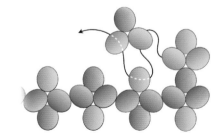

14 Snuggle up!

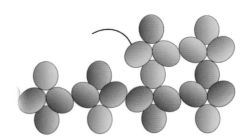

15 3rd stitch – **Phase 1**: This is a normal upright Hubble stitch. Pick up 2B, backstitch through the next head bead of the foundation row, and continue on through the 1st B bead picked up (in the same direction as before, making a ring).

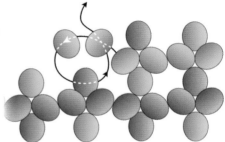

16 Snuggle up. **Phase 2**: Pick up 1B and pass down through the adjacent arm bead.

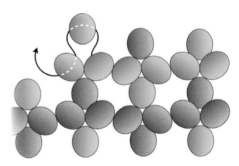

17 Snuggle up.

The next Hubble you make will be inverted, so work as for steps 11–14.

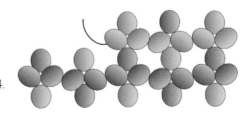

18 Continue working upright and inverted Hubbles alternately until the row is complete.

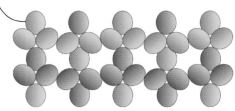

Step up as normal.

Heads up! Look at those lovely wavy lines in the beadwork and note the body beads of every other stitch, all set up, ready for the next row, which will revert back to the same colour scheme as in the foundation row.

Just to be sure you've got it, here's the pick-up sequence for the first 2 stitches of the 3rd row:

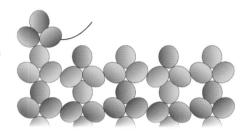

19 1st stitch (upright) – **Phase 1**: pick up 2A; **Phase 2**: pick up 1A. In shorthand that's 2A+1A.

20 2nd stitch (inverted) – **Phase 1**: pick up 2A,1B; pass again through the 1st A picked up in the same direction and complete the stitch by passing forward through the next body bead (which becomes the new head bead).

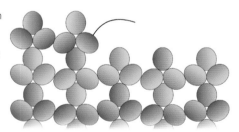

21 Repeat these stitches until the row is complete.

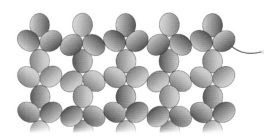

When I first discovered Wave Hubble I only had one tube of size 15° beads with me at the time, so I learned to make it tiny and in one colour! I was totally taken aback with how soft and delicate the piece felt and kept holding it up to the sky to look at the silhouette it made. So it's worth noting that working Wave Hubble in one colour produces a very beautiful textile in its own right, and you just have to have a go at working it in size 15°s!

As soon as I got back to my stash, I grabbed a contrasting colour to see where that would take me; I worked vertical stripes by using one colour for the upright stitches and the contrast for the inverted ones. This really highlights the fact that the stitches are heading in opposite directions, and always makes me think of M C Escher's intricate tessellation patterns, which led me to design the first WH project.

Once you've played with waves and stripes in your WH, try changing bead sizes within the row. The necklace on page 102 was worked by Nitty Chamcheon. Its beautiful, curving undulations beside the rivolis were achieved by working every WH row in 3 different sizes of bead. This is a similar concept to the Spex Vortex in *Let's Hubble!*

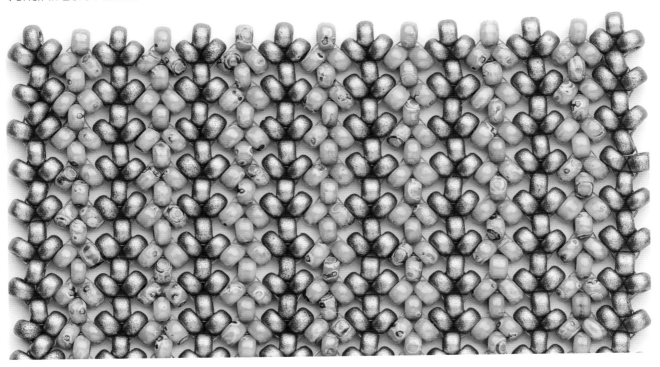

Now you've had a chance to get to know basic WH, it's time to have a little play with changing the colours of the bead positions within the stitches. The Metamorphose cuff is worked entirely in Wave Hubble and looks simple and straightforward at first glance but it presents little challenges along the way. As you build the rows, the colours will morph from the waves you have already practised, to vertical stripes, which will stop one by one, leaving only one colour, then you will gradually re-build the stripes and convert them back to waves! It's a great way of getting to know the 'anatomy' of WH, that is, which colour bead to pick up within the structure of each stitch. If you are familiar with creating patterns and images in peyote stitch, then you will understand the need for forward planning, in other words, sometimes you have to think a row or two ahead. This will become clear as you work the pattern. If it helps you to work from an image, read the one below from L-R. These instructions create a vertically built cuff of 50 rows, 16.5cm/6½" in length, but you can easily modify this by adding more rows (2 rows add 8mm/5/16") at the beginning, end and/or middle. Last quick tip - don't forget to step up at the end of every row.

This is my very humble homage to a work by M C Escher, whose surrealism and genius for detail I have always adored.

I chose bright, shiny, silver beads and beautiful, matte, charcoal grey iris ones to provide a stark contrast and make it easy to identify the individual beads within each stitch. It also looks great and rather chic. For help with the abbreviated pick-up sequences, see 'Pick up abbreviations' in Notes on page 4 for a full explanation.

What you will need:

- 7g x size 11° seed beads (metallic) (A)
- 8g x size 11° seed beads (matte) (B)
- 14 x size 15° seed beads (to match clasp and daisy spacers)
- 14 x daisy spacers (to complement the seed beads and clasp)
- 1 x 7-loop magnetic sliding clasp

Foundation Row:

1. Using A as the main colour and B for the body beads, cast on 13 Basic WH stitches. Pick-up sequence 2A, 1B+1A.

2nd Row:

2. Work this row using B as the main colour and A for the body beads. The repeating pick-up sequences for the first two stitches, will be as follows: 1st stitch: 2B+1B; 2nd stitch: 2B,1A.

Work the 3rd and 4th rows, continuing the alternating colours theme.

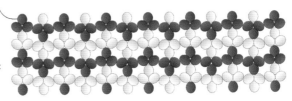

5th Row:

3. 1st stitch: 2B+1B; 2nd stitch: 3A. Work the rest of the row as normal with the main colour A and body beads B, by repeating the sequence: 2A+1A; 2A,1B.

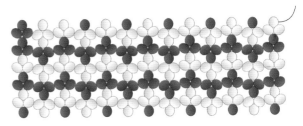

6th Row:

④ Work 11 stitches (main colour B, body beads A). 12th stitch: 3A; 13th stitch: 2B+1B.

7th Row:

⑤ 1st stitch: 2B+1B; 2nd stitch: 3A; 3rd stitch: 2B+1B; 4th stitch: 3A. Work the rest of the row as normal (main colour A, body beads B).

8th-16th Rows:

⑥ Continue morphing the horizontal waves into vertical stripes over the next 9 rows, until all the stitches alternate in colour at the end of the 16th row.

17th Row:

⑦ Repeat Row 16.

18th Row:

8　Begin phasing out the silver stripes. 1st stitch: 2B+1B; 2nd stitch: 3B; maintain the vertical stripes for the rest of the row.

19th Row:

9　Maintain the vertical stripes for 9 stitches. Work stitches 10-13 in B only.

20th-24th Rows:

10　Continue terminating one silver stripe on each row. The 23rd and 24th rows are worked entirely in B.

25th Row:

11　Now let's re-start the stripes at the other edge of the band. Work 12 stitches in B. 13th stitch: 2B+1A.

26th Row:

12　1st stitch: 2A+1A; 2nd stitch: 3B; 3rd stitch 2B+1A. Work remaining 10 stitches in B.

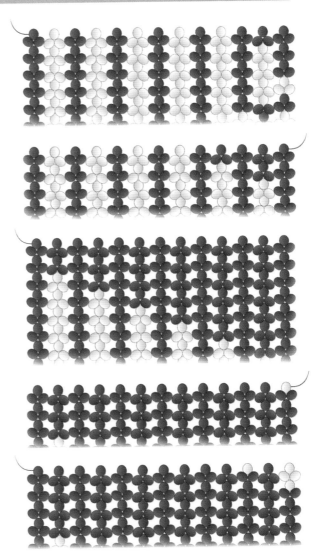

27th-32nd Rows:

13 Continue re-starting one silver stripe in each of the next 6 rows.

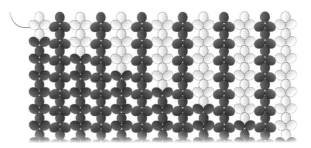

33rd-34th Rows:

14 Work 2 rows maintaining the stripes, then we'll start morphing the stripes back into waves.

35th Row:

15 1st stitch: 2B+1B; 2nd stitch: 2B,1A. Complete the row maintaining the stripes.

36th Row:

16 Work 11 stitches, maintaining the stripes. 12th stitch: 2A, 1B; 13th stitch: 2A+1A.

37th Row:

17 1st stitch: 2B+1B; 2nd stitch: 2B,1A; Repeat the 1st and 2nd stitches once more, then complete the row, maintaining the stripes.

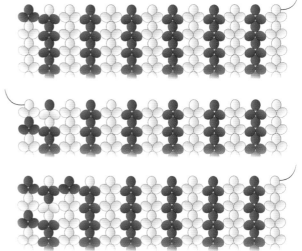

38th Row:

18 Work 9 stitches, maintaining the stripes. 10th stitch: 2A, 1B; 11th stitch: 2A+1A.

Repeat the 10th and 11th stitches once more, to complete the row.

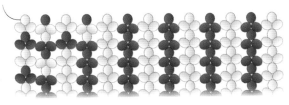

39th Row:

19 1st stitch: 2B+1B; 2nd stitch: 2B,1A. Repeat the 1st and 2nd stitches twice more, then complete the row maintaining the stripes.

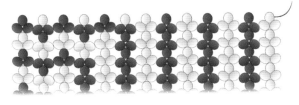

40th-46th Rows:

20 Continue morphing one vertical stripe into a wave as per the pick-up sequences you have been using in rows 35-39. The 46th row will be a complete wave in main colour A, with body beads B.

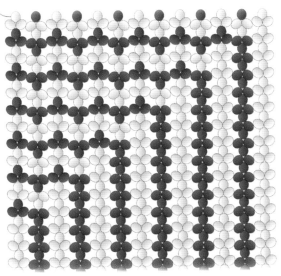

47th-50th Rows:

21 Continue the alternating coloured waves theme as for the first 4 rows, to mirror the other end of the cuff.

22 Attach the clasp as shown in *Let's Hubble!*, using daisy spacers, each anchored by a size 15° seed bead to cover the loops of the clasp.

Variations

- The first variation to be considered has to be bead colour and finish. Metamorphose was made with shiny beads to contrast with a matte finish and a dark colour contrasting with light. Try working in different finishes, for example mix Aurora Borealis (AB) with opaque, or transparent with metallic.

- I love the central section of just one colour as it subtly shows off the waves. Try working Wave Hubble in your favourite bead colour. Hmmm, now what's my favourite? Maybe the wonderful matte, earthy #2035 or gorgeous, golden iris #462 or beautiful light bronze #457L or...

- Bring in more colours or even carefully graduate shades of one colour across the band. Remember that the body bead of an inverted Hubble will become the head bead of the inverted Hubble in the following row, so you will have to think ahead. You could create a fabulous subtle effect of shifting waves and stripes this way.

- You don't have to follow my waves and stripes design, try doing your own thing like Erika Simons has done in her electric metallics cuff, with a central square motif – she's also gone a step further and used Travelling Waves which you'll meet in the next chapter. Erika Fidler did her own thing too and made the red and white cuff opposite, topped off with a Hubbled cabochon!

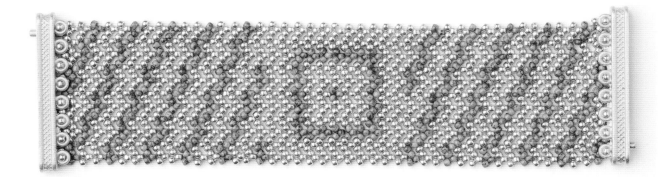

- As I said at the beginning of the project, this cuff is built vertically, but remember you can make a horizontal version by casting on enough Wave Hubbles to span your wrist (an odd number, don't forget), then build the width of the cuff with each row.

CHAPTER TWO

· · ·

Picture Wave Hubble

CHAPTER TWO

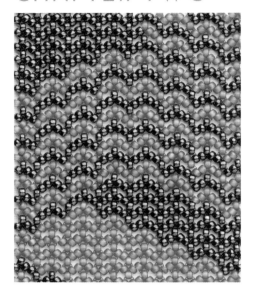

Picture Wave Hubble

If you've worked through Metamorphose you'll be getting to know the anatomy of a Hubble stitch and the effects of manipulating the colour positioning for the 4 beads that it comprises. In this chapter we'll explore this to a much greater level with the help of some travelling waves and a selfie!

The day after I made the very first WH swatch, I picked it up again to re-examine it and in a flash I could not only see the waves and stripes potential, but also what I now call 'travelling waves'. Once I'd had a little think with pen and paper as to how to start them off, I got cracking. Bear in mind that at that moment in time I was beading whilst bobbing along happily on the Solent in a little boat, surrounded by sparkling waves – a very big influence. It was when we had sailed around the Bay of Biscay and I spotted the Pyrenees off the north coast of Spain for the first time, that I was moved to try working a picture in Wave Hubble. The sloping sides of the mountains, the waves, clouds and even the sea birds all provided inspiration to give it a go.

If you were to draw an outline around a Hubble stitch, using a ruler, the resulting shape would be roughly that of a kite, not quite a diamond. So the different angles you get from the four facets of a Hubble stitch produce some interesting possibilities when making pictures.

To fully get to grips with the anatomy of a Hubble, let's take a close look at one. With the tail thread on the left, the first 2 beads picked up are the arms (1st is left, 2nd is right), the 3rd is the body bead, then in **Phase 2**, the 4th is the head.

The next Hubble will be inverted, which can confuse things as to which colour bead is going where when you are making patterns. Two useful facts to remember are:

1. The first bead picked up in **Phase 1** sits snugly against the arm bead of the previous Hubble.

2. The 3rd bead picked up in **Phase 1** is always the body bead (with one, teeny, little exception which you'll meet in the next chapter).

Travelling Waves

This was the easiest way to describe a wave pattern that appears to travel upwards diagonally as you add rows. Dependant upon which order you pick up the beads, you can make the waves travel either to the right or to the left. You can even get them to travel upwards diagonally from both sides of the beaded strip and meet in the middle. Hence, I wanted to make some mountains – well, it would've been rude not to!

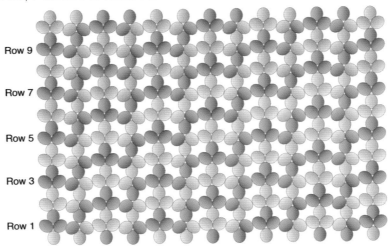

As you can see, the waves in this grid are travelling up to the right and, at first glance, this pattern may look highly complex, but let's break it down a little. Look closely at the 13 stitches of Row 1; there is a 4-stitch sequence repeated across the row. With green as A and lilac as B, here are the pick-up details for the repeating 4-stitch sequences in the first 3 rows:

Row 1 (Foundation Row) (L-R):	1) 2A,1B+1A
	2) 1A,1B,1A+1B
	3) 2B,1A+1B
	4) 1B,1A,1B+1A
Row 2 (R-L):	1) 2B+1B
	2) 1B,2A
	3) 2A+1A
	4) 1A,2B
Row 3 (L-R):	1) 2A+1A
	2) 1A,1B,1A
	3) 2B+1B
	4) 1B,1A,1B

You may also note that Rows 3, 5, 7 and 9 have identical repeating sequences and Rows 2, 4, 6, 8 and 10 also have their own identical repeating sequences. (We'll ignore the foundation row, as you'll always have to pick up 4 beads for each stitch, but you can still see the pattern there.) Basically what that all means is that once you've got to grips with Rows 1, 2 and 3, you just keeping repeating Rows 2 and 3.

To make your waves travel up to the left instead, hold a little mirror at the side of the diagram, or take a photo of it and/or scan it as a jpg file and then reverse it. Yes, I know you could cheat and just turn the beadwork over, but that wouldn't give you practice with the different sequences that you'll need for later project suggestions.

These waves radiate upwards from the sides of the strip and meet in the middle. The pick-up sequences will obviously change at the halfway point within each row, but, as before, once you have worked the first 3 rows, simply repeat rows 2 and 3 over and over, and a rhythm will start to flow as the pattern emerges.

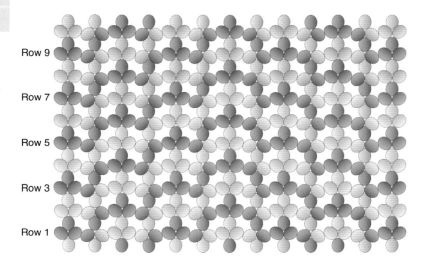

Row 9
Row 7
Row 5
Row 3
Row 1

Yes, it's me! Using a small grid (11 stitches by 17 rows), I worked a simple image of my face (on a good hair day). It was fun to do and, as it was quite a small piece, didn't take very long to make. The grid I used is below, and there's a blank grid for you to experiment with at the back of the book. Work in bead sizes 15°, 11° or 8°, but you will find that the smaller the beads you use, the neater and more detailed the image appears.

What you will need:

- 2g x seed beads (background)
- < 1g x seed beads (for each of face and hair)
- 5 x seed beads for mouth
- 2 x seed beads for eyes
- 2 x seed beads for earrings

Variations

- Play with the Wave Hubble grid on page 106 and see what other repeating patterns you can pick out.

- If you like the idea of the selfie in WH, why not do one for each member of your family.

- Photocopy the grid and draw out your designs. Calculate the number of rows you would need to span your wrist and work your family images into that number. The strip would grow vertically completing each image before starting a new one.

- Try a horizontal version – a little more challenging, where you cast on enough stitches to span the wrist, and gradually build all the family selfie images at once.

- Add interesting features like glasses, a moustache or dangly earrings, onto the surface as embellishments.

- Make a lovely bookmark as a gift for a friend or family member. Work a long strip in one or more colours, with or without stripes, waves or travelling waves and add the person's image somewhere along the strip. Add crystal fringes or dangles onto the beads at the bottom end – maybe straight, slanting or in V-formation.

- You may want to get a little more ambitious and try an entire scene! You can clearly see the mountains in my Atlantic View bracelet on page 24. I like the fact that the mountains aren't perfect and have slightly erratically sloping sides – that gives it a more organic feel.

- If you want even greater definition of outlines, try working in size 15°s.

- If, like me, you are a stickler for punishment, try working a small piece in size 15° Czech Charlottes. The fact that these beads are not just smaller but, proportionally, much narrower than Japanese seed beads, has the effect of making an extremely beautiful and even more lacy textile, where the gaps between the stitches play more of a role.

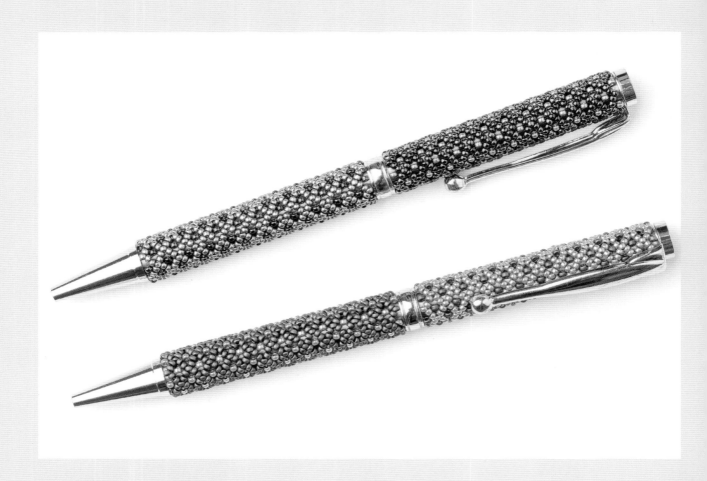

CHAPTER THREE

...

Interference Wave Hubble

CHAPTER THREE

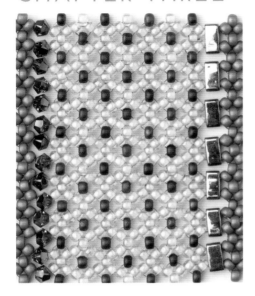

Interference Wave Hubble

This fun variation of Basic Wave Hubble was the next exploratory step that I took. It was so obvious, and you may be able to see why from this image. Interference Wave Hubble (IWH) has the appearance of 5-bead netting with what almost looks like a floating bead set in the centre of each diamond shape. However, unlike netting, IWH doesn't have springy, concertina-like movement, it produces a beaded fabric that holds its shape.

So far you've learnt that when you work each row of Basic WH you simply stitch an upright stitch on top of an upright stitch, and an inverted one on top of an inverted one. For IWH it's the opposite – you make an inverted stitch on top of an upright one and an upright stitch on top of an inverted one. Simple! But before you dash off and grab the beads to have a go, read on.

It was hard to decide where to put this chapter in the book because IWH doesn't quite conform to the norm, and here's why. What makes it different is that when you step up, the thread emerges in the wrong direction, making it impossible to begin a new row (Just like VerSO1 for normal Hubble). The solution is to work it in circular/tubular mode, or to work it in linear mode you can use the HorSO technique as I have done in the panel shown in the image: you can also try it out that way in Project 6, Chapter 5 (page 67).

Right, armed with that information, let's have a go. When working IWH, I like to use a contrast colour for the central bead to make it really stand out; it'll also help you to focus on which stitch you're about to make, so choose 2 contrasting colours, A and B.

Foundation Row:

1 Using A (main) and B (body bead), cast on an even number of stitches (for this swatch, let's say 12 – it's a good practice size to hold easily). Bring the two ends together as in the diagram.

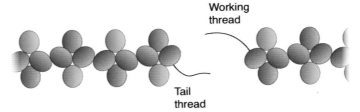

Working thread

Tail thread

2 Look carefully at where the tail thread is emerging and pass the needle up into that arm bead and on through the head bead as in the diagram. Snuggle up.

Workshop Tip 6: You've already encountered the circular/tubular Hubble join in book 1, *Let's Hubble!*, and this is exactly the same; a single thread coming from under their touching arms connects two consecutive Hubble stitches within a row to one another, so when you join two ends of beadwork together, the join must look and function the same as every other join. Even if one of those Hubbles is inverted, the thread pathway is exactly the same.

3 As the join will be very loose, secure it by passing around this Hubble and snuggling up. I'll dispense with the tail thread in the diagrams from now on.

Heads up! The Hubble from which the thread is emerging is an upright one, so, as this is IWH, we are going to build an inverted one onto it.

2nd Row:

4 Pick up 1A,1B,1A and pass through all 3 again, making the body base.

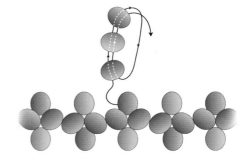

Workshop Tip 7: Important fact: Here's a great time to let you know a Hubble stitch rule. When working an inverted Hubble, the 3rd bead picked up in Phase 1 is always the body bead, with one exception, which is that if the inverted stitch is the first stitch of a new row, the 2nd of the 3 beads picked up will be the body bead, and you must pass through all 3 beads again; this goes for both Hubble and WH forms. If you are working the 2-Drop and 3-Drop forms, the body bead has to be the middle one picked up and you must pass through all the beads picked up once more (5 beads for 2-Drop and 7 for 3-Drop).

5 Holding your beadwork exactly as in the diagram, with the thread emerging from the left side of the foundation row head bead, pass through the head bead from right to left.

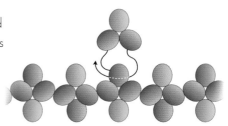

6 Pass through the adjacent arm bead to complete the stitch and snuggle up.

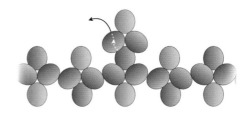

7 Using A only, work an upright Hubble onto the body bead of the next foundation Hubble.

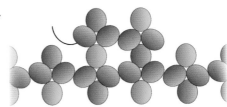

8 Pick up 2A,1B for the next stitch, which is inverted. We're back to the normal pick-up sequence for inverted Hubbles where the 3rd bead is the body bead.

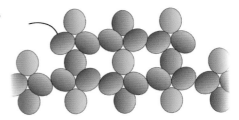

9 Repeat steps 7-8 until the row is complete. To join the last stitch, which will be upright, onto the first stitch, which is inverted, you must pass downwards into the arm from above and on into the head bead below. Step up to emerge from the body bead of that first inverted stitch. The 3rd row will commence with an upright stitch on top of the inverted one.

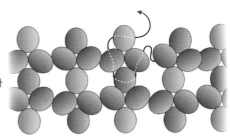

These craft pens showcase IWH perfectly and work up quite quickly so they're great to make as gifts. It's fun playing with contrasting colours in the two beadable sections; use one colour as main and the other as the body bead, as you've already practised, but then swap them over; both complement each other and produce a very different look. I suggest working the section nearest the pen tip first, as there's no clip obstacle to negotiate whilst you're getting used to working the stitch on a solid core.

What you will need:

- 1 x Slimline Beadable Pen

- 4g x size 15° Miyuki seed beads (A)

- 4g x size 15° Miyuki seed beads (B)

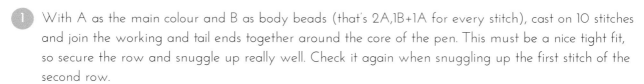

1. With A as the main colour and B as body beads (that's 2A,1B+1A for every stitch), cast on 10 stitches and join the working and tail ends together around the core of the pen. This must be a nice tight fit, so secure the row and snuggle up really well. Check it again when snuggling up the first stitch of the second row.

2. Work 22 rows in IWH and finish off both the tail and working threads.

3. With B as main and A as body beads, repeat steps 1 and 2 for the top half of the pen, taking care not to snag the thread around the pen clip when you get to that level. A good way of avoiding it is to constantly rotate the beadwork around the core as you work it. You can also bend the clip away from the beadwork very slightly, but don't allow it to bang back against them, as it can smash the beads.

Variations

- There are quite a few beadable objects available, for example key rings, letter openers, needle cases and unpickers, so you have plenty of opportunities to play with IWH.

- Work out your own colour scheme and have a go at making patterns such as a virtual 'basket weave' with the diagonals that manifest in this technique. Take a look at the close-up of a section of the Outer Limits Cuff on page 65.

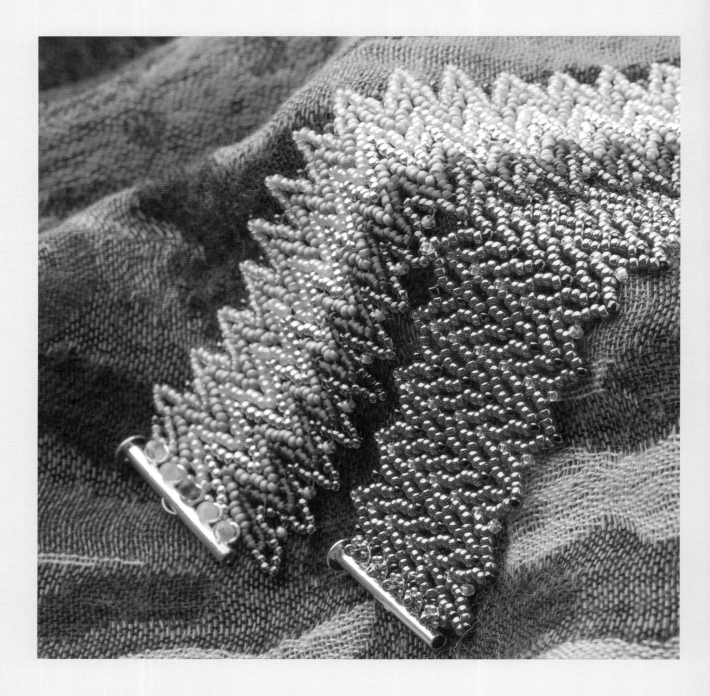

CHAPTER FOUR

•••

2-Drop, 3-Drop Wave Hubble

and transitions

CHAPTER FOUR

2-Drop Wave Hubble

Of course the logical progression for my frenzied journey of discovery was to try 2-Drop and then 3-Drop Wave Hubble, all of which happened in one day, with the same size 15 beads. I was bowled over by the results and couldn't wait to get back to my stash and try more. Interestingly, Basic WH rows have pretty smooth straight starting and finishing edges, however, as soon as the stitch becomes larger, as with 2- and 3-Drop, the row edges undulate to greater and greater degrees. We'll use a different colour for the body bead, as we did in Chapter 1 for Basic WH stitch, to facilitate learning the technique.

2-Drop Wave Foundation Row:

1. Work a 2-Drop Hubble, picking up 4A,1B for the body ring, then 1A for the head (4A,1B+1A).

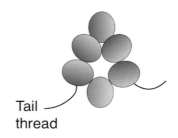

Tail thread

2. Work a second stitch and snuggle it up firmly to the first stitch. The second stitch will flip upside down.

    The arm beads of the 2 stitches should have their holes pressed against each other, with no visible thread between them.

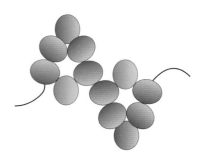

3 Work some more stitches, finishing with an odd number, so that the last 2-Drop Hubble is upright, and step up to emerge from the head bead, as normal.

Heads up! Just a quick view of the real life foundation row of 2-Drop stitches.

2nd Row: It's time to switch colours.

4 1st stitch – **Phase 1**: Pick up 4B and make the body ring by passing through the head bead of the 2-Drop Foundation Hubble below.

5 Still in **Phase 1**: Continue on through the first 2 beads of the 4 just picked up and snuggle up.

6 **Phase 2**: Pick up 1B and position the head by passing down through the adjacent two beads.

7 2nd stitch: Work an inverted 2-Drop Hubble thus: Pick up 4B,1A. Pass again through the first 2B picked up in the same direction, making a ring.

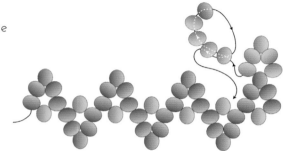

8 2nd stitch (cont.): Pass forward through the presenting body bead of the row below, and on through the 2 arm beads, as in the diagram.

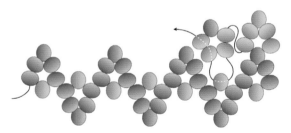

9 2nd stitch (cont.): Snuggle up, nice and tight! There must be no visible thread between the arms of the 2 stitches.

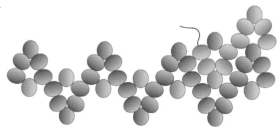

10 3rd stitch – **Phase 1**: Pick up 4B, backstitch through the next presenting foundation head bead, and continue on through the first two beads picked up, in the same direction as before, making the body ring.

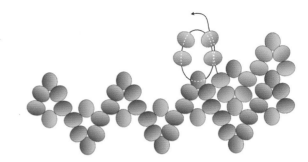

11 **Phase 2**: Snuggle up, then pick up 1B and pass down through the adjacent 2B to position the head bead.

12 Complete the row, alternating the upright and inverted stitches. Step up as normal.

13 The 3rd row will be worked in exactly the same way, but with the colours reversed again.

3-Drop Wave Hubble

The 3-Drop version creates a more exaggerated zig-zagging wave and, to me, when worked in a single colour produces wonderful textural patterns. In fact, I thoroughly recommend trying all Wave Hubbles in a single colour once you've mastered the techniques, as they look and feel like material; superb on their own or as a textured background for embellishing – think evening bags, purses, spectacles cases or even a waistcoat, as one of my students has planned to make!

3-Drop Wave Foundation Row:

1 Work a 3-Drop Hubble, picking up 6A,1B for the body ring, then 1A for the head (6A,1B+1A).

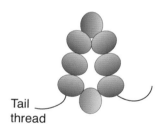

Tail thread

2 Work a second stitch and snuggle up tight to the first stitch, flipping the 2nd stitch upside down.

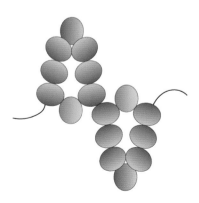

3 Work a row of stitches, ending with an odd number, and step up as normal, to emerge from the head bead.

And here's the real 3-Drop foundation row...

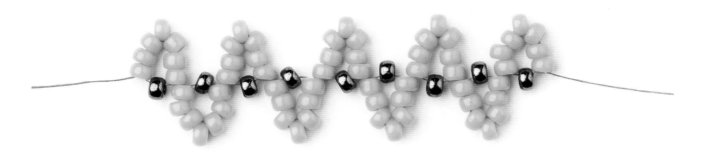

2nd Row:

4 1st stitch: Using B as the main colour for this row, work a 3-Drop Hubble for the 1st stitch (picking up 6B+1B).

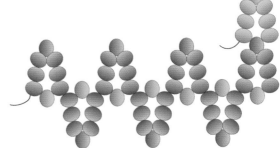

5 2nd stitch: Work an inverted 3-Drop Hubble thus: pick up 6B,1A; pass again through the first 3B picked up in the same direction, making a ring.

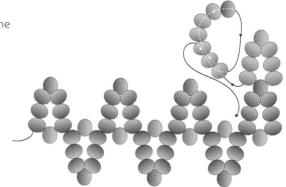

6 2nd stitch (cont.): Pass forward through the presenting body bead of the row below, and on through the 3 arm beads as in the diagram.

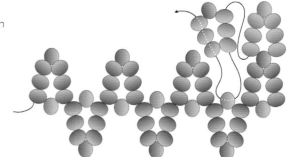

7 2nd stitch (cont.): Snuggle up nice and tight, as always.

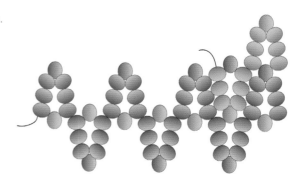

8 Complete the row, alternating the upright and inverted stitches. Step up as normal.

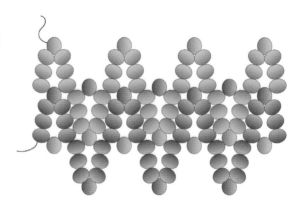

9 Continue working your swatch, alternating the row colours. Don't you just love those beautiful, long diagonals?

Erika Simons worked the two lovely cuffs on page 40. For the green one, she chose beads in seven different shades, and planned the shade sequence. Remember that it's necessary to think ahead to which colour you will use in the following row, because the body beads you use for the inverted Hubbles in the current row will become the head beads of the subsequent row. For the red cuff, Erika used a main, single colour throughout, but changed the colour for both the head and body beads.

Making the transition

The three versions of WH (Basic, 2-Drop and 3-Drop) can easily be morphed into one another. Moving row by row from Basic, through 2-Drop to 3-Drop causes the beadwork to fan out whilst the waves increase in depth. However, a 2-Drop WH row cannot be worked immediately on top of a Basic WH row as it produces a lumpy surface and sits rather unsatisfactorily.

The same applies to a 3-Drop row straight on top of a 2-Drop row. The solution is to work a transition row between a row of smaller stitches and a row of larger stitches.

Let's say you are morphing from Basic to 2-Drop WH; the transition row will consist of upright 2-Drop stitches alternating with inverted Basic stitches. So, it's a kind of halfway house – half of the stitches are the next size up and upright, and half are the same as the previous row and inverted. It therefore follows that to morph from 2-Drop to 3-Drop, your transition row will consist of upright 3-Drop stitches alternating with inverted 2-Drop stitches.

If that hasn't completely fried your brain, let's have a go! We'll still continue using the 2-colour system as it really helps to see that different coloured body bead and know that you're about to work an inverted stitch.

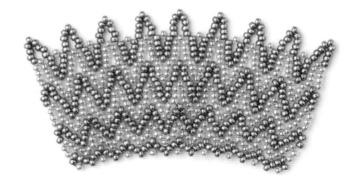

Foundation Row:

1 Work a foundation row in Basic WH, using A as the main colour and B for the body beads.

. Step up.

2nd Row (Transition):

2 1st stitch: Using B, work a 2-Drop Hubble.

3 2nd stitch: Pick up 2B,1A and work an inverted Basic Hubble.

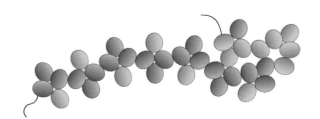

4 3rd stitch: Using B, work a 2-Drop Hubble.

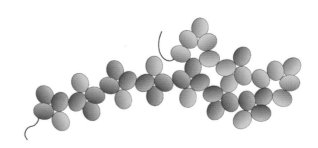

5 Repeat steps 3-4 to the end of the row and step up.

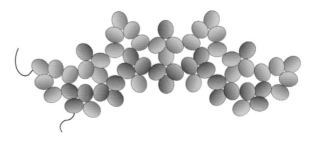

3rd Row:

6 Using A for the main and B for the body beads, work the entire row in 2-Drop WH.

From here on the diagrams roughly represent the appearance of the beadwork. In reality the stitches must all be beautifully snuggled up, with no thread visible between the arms of adjacent stitches.

4th Row (Transition):

7 Step up.

1st stitch: Using B, work a 3-Drop Hubble.

2nd stitch: Pick up 4B,1A and work an inverted 2-Drop Hubble.

Repeat this stitching pattern to the end of the row.

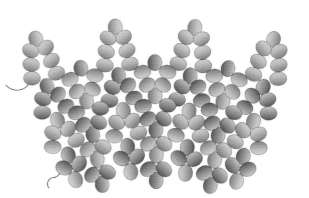

5th Row:

8 Using A for the main and B for the body beads, work the entire row in 3-Drop WH.

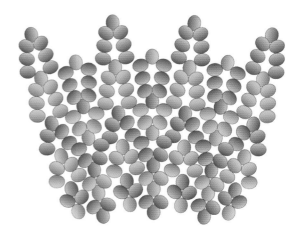

Morphing from Basic to 3-Drop Wave Hubble in 5 rows, fans out the beadwork quickly, as you can see. Working two or more of each normal WH row between the transition rows, fans out the beadwork more gently respectively, for example Rows 1 & 2: Basic; Row 3: Transition (Basic + 2-Drop); Rows 4 & 5: 2-Drop; Row 6: Transition (2-Drop + 3-Drop); Row 7: 3-Drop.

So, the more normal WH rows you work between the transition rows, the slower the curvature. Thus you can control the shaping of the beadwork, such as gently curving a design for a beaded collar, or fanning out fast at the beginning and slowing down towards the 3-Drop stage to shape a purse or bag.

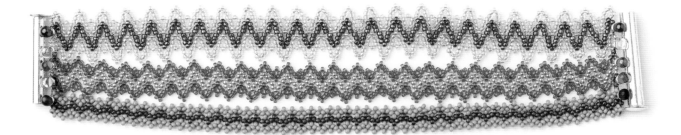

The electromagnetic spectrum is composed of waves of different sizes or frequencies. The visible portion of that spectrum, light and all its component colours, is so important to us beadworkers, so the name for this design was an obvious one when I'd completed it. Here's a great opportunity to practise all three WH stitch skills and have a play with colour tones or finishes. Frequency Bracelet is composed of 3 strips of WH – Basic, 2-Drop and 3-Drop, and each strip is just 3 rows wide. I chose to work with three different pairs of blue shades in size 15° seed beads for the Frequency Bracelet, but it can be worked in any size bead. The difference between what you've been practising so far and this project is that there are no body beads of a different colour in the foundation and 3rd rows, so the lovely wave along the centre really stands out.

What you will need:

- 2g x size 15° seed beads in each of A, C, E & F
- 1g x size 15° seed beads in each of B & D
- 10 x Magatama Drop beads (to match or complement A-F)
- 1 x 5-loop magnetic sliding clasp (or your chosen clasp)

Basic WH strip:

1. With a good wingspan of thread, leaving a tail thread of 20cm/8" and using colours A & B, cast on the foundation row of Basic WH thus: 1st stitch: 3A+1A; 2nd stitch 2A,1B+1A. Repeat these two stitches until the foundation row spans your wrist (remember the clasp will add another 1cm/1/2" to the overall length). Make sure you finish with an odd number, so that the last stitch is upright like the 1st stitch. Check your foundation row to make sure that only the inverted Hubbles have body beads in colour B.

2. Step up and work the 2nd row, using B for the main and A for the body beads: 1st stitch: 2B+1B; 2nd stitch: 2B,1A. Keep repeating these two stitches until you have completed the row.

3. Step up and work the 3rd row; you will only be working in A, thus: 1st stitch: 2A+1A; 2nd stitch: 3A. Keep repeating these two stitches until you have completed the row. Pass once more around the final stitch of the row to secure it but don't finish off. Weave around to emerge from the end arm bead of the 2nd row.

4. Attach this end of the strip to a loop on the clasp, using a drop bead as an anchor. Weave back into the strip and take up all the slack in the thread, so none is visible and the drop bead is sitting tightly in the loop. Finish off. Using the tail thread, do the same for the other end of the strip on the corresponding clasp loop.

2-Drop WH strip:

5. Work this strip in the same way as for the Basic one, using colours C and D. As the 2-Drop stitch is wider than Basic, you cannot work the same number of stitches, so you must simply cast on enough stitches (once again an odd number) to match the length of the first strip. Check that for the foundation row only the inverted stitches have a body bead in colour D.

6. When attaching the clasp, you must use two loops for each end of this strip.

3-Drop WH strip:

7 Work this strip in the same way as the other two, using E and F. Again, cast on an odd number of stitches to match the length of the other two strips. Check the foundation row to ensure that only your inverted stitches have body beads in colour F.

8 Use the remaining two loops on each side of the clasp for the final attachments.

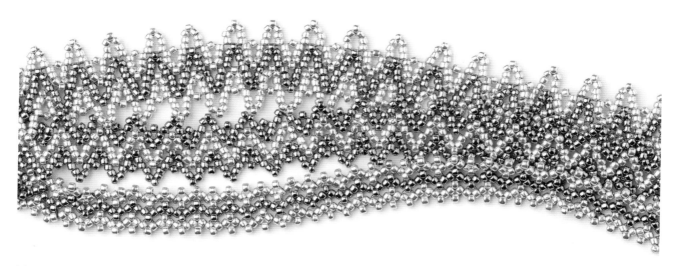

Variations

- You may prefer to work all three strips in the same 2 colours. Nitty made the bracelet shown above and reversed the colours on the 2-Drop strip.

- Work individual strips as little friendship bracelets, or make long strips as braided trims to spruce up a lampshade.

- If working in size 11° seed beads, try substituting matching mini drop beads on the foundation row for the head beads of inverted Hubbles, and on the 3rd row for the head beads of the upright Hubbles, so that both edges of the strip are bobbly.

When I first made these I was instantly reminded of our Moroccan rug in the living room, so I was possibly subliminally influenced by it, hence the title Kelim. A feature I rather like is the centre of the pattern, which looks like an eye. Although the Kelim earrings design is quite a small project, the techniques will take you to further heights in your experience of WH. You'll not only be working faster transitions from Basic to 3-Drop WH, but also each row begins with an inverted stitch, so your step up will be different.

Each earring is worked in 2 halves; you'll work the upper half first, then weave back down to the starting point and work the 2nd half, finally adding the dangles and the ear-wire loop.

What you will need:

- 0.5g x size 11° seed beads in each of A, B & C

- 0.5g x size 15° seed beads (to match A) (D)

- 6 x Crystal Drop beads (to complement chosen beads) (E)

- 1 x pair ear wires (to tone with beads)

Foundation Row:

The body bead of the 2nd stitch will position the 'eye'.

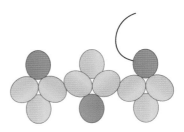

1. With 1.5m/60" thread and leaving a tail thread of 20cm/8" work the foundation row thus: 1st stitch: 2A,1B+1A; 2nd stitch: 2A,1C+1A; 3rd stitch: 2A,1B+1A.

   NB: Hold your beadwork so that the 1st and 3rd stitches are inverted, and the 2nd is upright.

   Step up simply by passing through the body bead, to emerge as in the diagram.

2nd Row - Transition (Basic - 2-Drop):

Remember the 1st stitch of the row is inverted, so this is no ordinary inverted stitch. For a quick reminder of how it's done check steps 4–6, page 36.

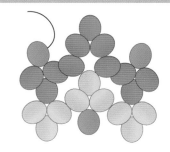

2 1st stitch (Basic, inverted): 1B,1C,1B; 2nd stitch (2-Drop, upright): 4B+B; 3rd stitch (Basic, inverted): 2B,1C.

Step up to emerge from the body bead.

3rd Row - Transition (2-Drop-3-Drop):

Again the 1st stitch of the row is inverted (and therefore special), but this time it's a 2-Drop Hubble, so you need to pick up a total of 5 beads (not 3 as for Basic) and pass through all 5 again before passing through the head bead of the row below.

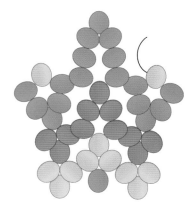

3 1st stitch (2-Drop, inverted): 2C,1A,2C; 2nd stitch (3-Drop, upright): 6C+1C; 3rd stitch (2-Drop, inverted): 4C,1A.

Step up to emerge from the body bead.

4 Turn the beadwork upside down and follow the threadpath on the diagram to emerge from the head bead of the 1st stitch of the foundation row.

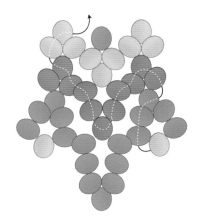

5   Now you're ready to work the same 3 rows from this base. The only difference is that the foundation row is already there, so the next row is worked thus:

1st stitch (Basic inverted): 1A,1B,1A; 2nd stitch (Basic, upright): 2A+1A; 3rd stitch (Basic, inverted): 2A,1B. Now you've got that lovely eye in the centre!

6   Repeat step 2.

7   Repeat step 3.

8   Now let's add the dangles. Turn the beadwork so the last row is at the bottom. The diagram only represents the lower half of the beadwork.

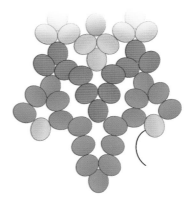

9   a) Pick up 1D,1E,3D and pass back through E and the 1st D picked up in the opposite direction.

     b) Pass through the body bead of the 2-Drop stitch, via the side where no thread is emerging.

     c) Snuggle up the dangle.

     d) Weave through to emerge from the head bead of the central 3-Drop stitch by following the threadpath in the diagram.

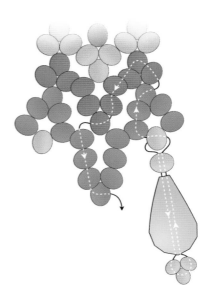

10 Make the 2nd dangle, same as the first, then follow the threadpath in the diagram to emerge from the body bead of the 2-Drop stitch, ready to place the last dangle.

11 Make the 3rd dangle as before, and finish off the working thread.

Now we're going to make the tiny loop for attachment to the ear-wires.

12 With the tail thread, weave through to emerge from the head bead of the central 3-Drop stitch.

13 Pick up 9D and pass through the head bead again in the same direction.

14 Pass through all 9D and the head bead again. Snuggle up.

15 Weave down into the stitches below and finish off the tail thread.

Now all you have to do is make its partner!

Variations

- Scale them down one size of beads for a pretty, petite pair like the black, white and silver earrings opposite. Try dagger beads or 3mm bicones or a combination of both for more spectacular dangles!

- I really like that eye at the centre and I think it could be exploited by working the design in some wonderful Egyptian colours – gold, lapis lazuli blue, coral and turquoise...

- Picture the Kelim motif on its side without the loop and dangles; it could be repeated a number of times to make a bracelet. Each time you make a new motif, instead of picking up a new head bead on one half, you could share the head bead of the central 3-Drop stitch on the previous motif to grow the bracelet.

CHAPTER FIVE

...

HorSO Wave Hubble

HorSO Wave Hubble

Just because WH stitches are tightly snuggled up to one another, it doesn't mean you can't fit a bead or crystal in between, and the simplicity of the HorSO technique remains exactly so. For WH, HorSO is executed in exactly the same way as for normal Hubble, that is, work a stitch, pick up the spacer bead plus the beads for the next stitch, ignore the spacer bead and work the next stitch. HorSO brings so much more potential to all forms of Hubble stitch; thus far I've identified the following four advantages:

- Spacer beads are fun to introduce into your beadwork; they look fabulous and they can provide an exciting break in large blocks of stitches. A gorgeous crystal adjacent to contrasting beads really stands out, or next to similar colour beads gives a surprising twinkle as the beadwork moves. You can make a great visual statement using the contrast between the ruler-straight edge of Tila and Half-Tila beads beside the soft, rounded edges of seed beads. Whilst not a problem, it is worthy of note that the thread passing from one stitch to the next in normal Hubble lies in a straight line, so a spacer bead on that thread will lie in that same straight line. However, the thread between two WH stitches lies at an angle of about 45°, so when you add a spacer bead, it too will lie at an angle. The larger the spacer bead, the more the angle appears to diminish, as the stitches are pushed further apart. 2-hole beads, like Tilas, tend not to show the angle, as the 2 holes compensate for each other.

- HorSO widens beadwork – that's obvious! But, it's also important to point out that if the spacer beads are the same as the beads you are using for the actual stitches, not only do they blend in imperceptibly with the waves, softening their zig-zaginess, but, of course, they also add an extra bead to every stitch. If you have a large area to cover or long length to achieve, gaining the width of 10 beads for every 10 stitches makes a considerable difference to beading time and still looks super. You'll find how to make these two WH ropes in Chapter 6; one is a simple 2-Drop and the other is the same number of stitches but in HorSO 2-Drop.

- Another reason to use the HorSO technique (whether for normal Hubble or WH) is as a method of increasing a row above a non-HorSO row, to make the beadwork fan out, and it provides a useful and interesting solution to adding that little bit of distance needed to get around a cabochon.

- Adding a spacer bead at the end of a row creates a very useful turning point when working IWH. In Chapter 3, I mentioned HorSO is a good solution to linear IWH and here's why. When you step up, you need the thread to be emerging away from the beadwork to continue with the next row, but with IWH it never will; placing a spacer bead at the end of a row does the trick. The image right illustrates this perfectly. The Outer Limits Cuff (Project 6) is worked in size 11° seed beads with pretty panels of IWH at each end of the cuff. To step up I placed a Half-Tila bead at each end of the foundation row and continued adding new ones as necessary each time I'd used both holes of the existing ones.

Here's how it's done:

At the end of a row, pass through one hole of a Tila or Half-Tila bead, and pick up 3 seed beads, then pass back through the 2nd hole of the Tila bead, thus changing direction. You are now totally independent of the stitch in the row below, so...

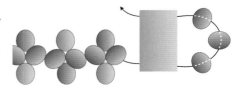

snuggle up and, either stitch an inverted Hubble for your new row of IWH or...

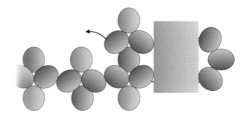

work an upright Hubble for normal WH. You can use the central bead of the 3 on the outer side of the Tila bead, as an anchor point when attaching a clasp.

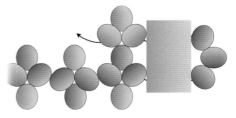

The cuff ends will be asymmetric because at the end of the 2nd row you will pass through the 2nd hole of the Tila bead and then need to pick up 3 seed beads and another Tila to begin the 3rd row. When the cuff is complete you can go back and tidy up both ends to mirror each other, by adding more beads outside the Tilas as necessary.

Workshop Tip 8: I need to add one huge reminder about HorSO when working in circular or tubular mode – don't forget to pick up the final HorSO bead at the end of a row before you join the end onto the beginning. I have to keep reminding myself, so I know how easy it is to forget.

As a child I was a great fan of the *Outer Limits* TV show, and loved the introduction, which depicted waves and apparent electrical interference in the broadcast, suggesting it came from an alien source. This cuff has both the travelling electrical waves and interference patterns – you can make them as live wire or soft and muted as you like. The Outer Limits Cuff is composed of 4 panels, with the 2 on the left mirroring the 2 on the right; the 2 inner panels are travelling waves in Basic WH, radiating towards the centre from both sides and the 2 outer panels are a pattern of IWH heading in opposite directions. The cuff length is 17cm/6¾" but if you need to lengthen the strip, work a swatch of a few rows first to familiarise yourself with the workings of this design, then work a fresh foundation row to your required length by adding stitches in twos evenly to panels along the length of the bracelet. If you only need an extra 12mm/½", simply substitute Tilas for the Half-Tilas. We'll call the panels (L-R) P1, P2, P3 and P4.

What you will need:

- 5g x size 11° seed beads (A – Opaque Cobalt Blue)

- 3g x size 11° seed beads (B – Opaque Light Turquoise)

- 11g x size 11° seed beads (C – Light Gold)

- 3g x size 11° seed beads (D – Salmon Pink)

- 28 x Half-Tila beads (E – Metallic Bronze AB)

- 7 x Tila beads (F – Turquoise Picasso)

- 8 x Drop beads (G)

- 8 x Dagger beads (H)

- 1 x 8-loop magnetic clasp (or your chosen clasp)

Foundation Row (When picking up the Tilas and Half-Tilas, only pass through one hole):

1. With a good wingspan and leaving a tail thread of 18cm/7", pick up 1C and pass through it again to make a stop bead.

2. Pick up 1E.

3. P1 (10 stitches in IWH) - *1st stitch: 1A,1B,1C+1A; 2nd stitch: 1B,1A,1C+1A.* Repeat from *to* 4 more times, completing 10 stitches in all.

4. Pick up 1E.

5. P2 (11 stitches in travelling waves) - *1st stitch: 2A,1C+1A; 2nd stitch: 1A,1C,1A+1C; 3rd stitch: 2C,1D+1C; 4th stitch: 1C,1D,1C+1D; 5th stitch: 2D,1A+1D;* 6th stitch: 1D,1A,1D+1A. Repeat the first 5 stitches working from *to*, completing 11 stitches in all.

6. Pick up 1F.

7. P3 (11 stitches in travelling waves) - *1st stitch: 2D,1A+1D; 2nd stitch: 1D,2C+1D; 3rd stitch: 2C,1D+1C; 4th stitch: 1C,2A+1C; 5th stitch: 2A,1C+1A;* 6th stitch: 1A,2D+1A. Repeat the first 5 stitches working from *to*, completing 11 stitches in all.

8. Pick up 1E.

9. P4 (10 stitches in IWH) - Work stitches as for step 3.

10. Pick up 1E,3C. Pass through the 2nd hole of the E bead in the opposite direction, to make a turn, ready for the 2nd row.

Heads up! Check all stitches are correctly snuggled and don't forget that the stitches can still flip over whilst beading, so you will still have to ask that very important question each time you are about to make a stitch!

2nd Row:

(11) P4 - Ensure the last stitch you made in the foundation row is upright, so, as this is IWH, the 2nd row will start with an inverted stitch (but it's not special because there's a spacer bead helping to start the row). *1st stitch: 1B,1A,1C; 2nd stitch: 1A,1B+1A.* Repeat from *to* 4 more times.

(12) Pass through the 2nd hole of the E bead.

(13) P3 - Ensure the awaiting foundation stitch is upright. As this is normal WH, start with an upright stitch. *1st stitch: 2D+1D; 2nd stitch: 1D,1A,1D; 3rd stitch: 2A+1A; 4th stitch: 1A,1C,1A; 5th stitch: 2C+1C;* 6th stitch: 1C,1D,1C. Repeat the first 5 stitches working from *to*, to complete the panel row - stitches 7-11 correspond to stitches 1-5.

(14) Pass through the 2nd hole of the F bead.

(15) P2 - Ensure the awaiting foundation stitch is upright as with P3 and we'll start with an upright stitch. *1st stitch: 2C+1C; 2nd stitch: 1C,2A; 3rd stitch: 2A+1A; 4th stitch: 1A,2D; 5th stitch: 2D+1D;* 6th stitch: 1D, 2C. Repeat the first 5 stitches working from *to*, to complete the panel row - stitches 7-11 correspond to stitches 1-5.

(16) Repeat step 12.

(17) P1 - Ensure the awaiting foundation stitch is inverted. The first stitch you make must be upright as this is IWH. *1st stitch: 1B,1A+1A; 2nd stitch: 1A,1B,1C.* Repeat from *to* 4 more times.

(18) Pass through the 2nd hole of the last E bead. Pick up 3C,1E.

3rd Row (No more asking the question, Yippee!):

(19) P1 - *1st stitch (upright): 1A,1B+1A; 2nd stitch: 1B,1A,1C.* Repeat from *to* 4 more times.

(20) Pick up 1E.

21) P2 - Work stitches 1-11 as for stitches 5, 6, 1, 2, 3, 4, 5, 6, 1, 2, 3, in step 13.

22) Pick up 1F.

23) P3 - Work stitches 1-11 as for stitches 3, 4, 5, 6, 1, 2, 3, 4, 5, 6, 1, in step 15.

24) Pick up 1E.

25) P4 - *1st stitch (inverted): 1A,1B,1C; 2nd stitch: 1B,1A+1A.* Repeat from *to* four more times.

26) Pick up 1E,3C. Pass through the 2nd hole of the E bead in the opposite direction.

4th Row:

27) P4 - Repeat steps 11 and 12.

28) P3 - Work stitches 1-11 as for stitches 3, 4, 5, 6, 1, 2, 3, 4, 5, 6, 1, in step 13.

29) Repeat step 14.

30) P2 - Work stitches 1-11 as for stitches 5, 6, 1, 2, 3, 4, 5, 6, 1, 2, 3, in step 15.

31) Repeat step 12.

32) P1 - Repeat steps 17 and 18.

33) By now you may be able to see the patterns emerging and recognise the repeating sequences. Maintaining the patterns in each panel, continue until you have completed 14 rows and finish off.

Now we need to equalise both ends of the cuff, as they are different. At the tail thread end the E beads are each joined together by 3C, and at the opposite end the E beads aren't joined together at all, but have 3C sitting on their outer edges.

34 Work a new thread into the opposite end of the cuff (not the tail thread end) and add 1C bead between each of the C beads sitting over the E bead holes thus:

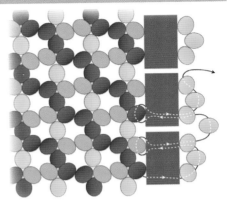

With the new thread emerging from the arm bead, A, of the foundation row end Hubble:

a) pass through E, and the 3C;

b) pass through the 2nd hole of the E bead and through B (of the Hubble).

c) Pass back through the 2nd hole of the E bead and through the closest C bead in the opposite direction to the first pass.

d) Pick up 1C;

e) pass through the 1st C bead on the next E bead and on through the E bead;

f) through A (of the Hubble), back through the 1st hole of the E bead, and the closest C bead in the opposite direction to the first pass;

g) through the next 2C to emerge as in the diagram.

h) Repeat steps b–g to place a C bead between every group of 3C.

35 At this point you must assess connection points to the clasp loops by holding the cuff and clasp side by side. It's really a case of easing it into the best fit – you have plenty of C beads available to use for the connections, both the new ones you just added and the central ones in the groups of 3. Once you know which C bead is closest to the first loop, weave into the cuff for security, then back out to emerge from the designated C bead.

36 Pass through the corresponding clasp loop, pick up 1C and pass back through the loop.

37 Snuggle up and weave on to emerge from the C bead closest to the next loop.

38 Repeat steps 36-37 until all 8 loops are attached.

39 Finish off.

40 Now let's complete the tail thread end. Remove the stop bead from the tail thread but don't finish it off just yet.

41 Work in a new thread and weave through to emerge where the tail thread is emerging.

42 Pick up 2C and pass down through the existing C bead sitting over the 2nd hole of the E bead and the E bead. Snuggle up.

43 Add C beads at this end to mirror the opposite end. From here on you'll be adding a central C bead to make the groups of 3C instead of a C bead between the groups of 3C, but the weaving will be very much the same.

44 Attach the remaining side of the clasp as for the first end.

45 Finish off the tail thread.

46 If desired, work simple or elaborate fringes in Basic or 2-Drop Hubble from each of the 16 C beads anchoring the cuff to the clasp loops.

Variations

- Where shall I start?! Use those Tilas or Half-Tilas to divide up the beadwork into as many or as few panels as you like. Make a fabulous patchwork of different stitch panels. In the green and blue cuff below, I've included not only WH and IWH, but also some normal Hubble!

- Narrow panels make quite dramatic beady statements like the 'Egyptian' cuff below.

- Work a cuff as a vertical strip instead of a horizontal one, and strategically place your favourite spacer beads one or two stitches in from the edges or between centre stitches on each row, to create interesting, defining lines.

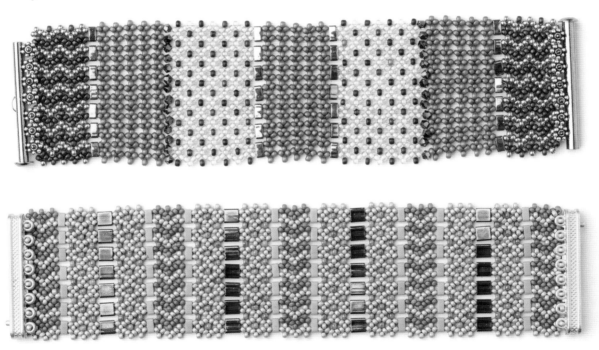

Pump up the volume - it's party time! To make sound louder you increase the amplitude of sound waves – they have the same frequencies but the waves become larger from peak to trough. That's pretty much what's happening in this design – well OK, there is a little spread, but indulge me! Working the HorSO technique for every row, using size 11° beads that match the row beads as the spacers, you will start with Basic WH and transition through to 3-Drop. The resulting curve of the beadwork is so gentle that it makes a cuff, beautifully tailored to the wrist and hand.

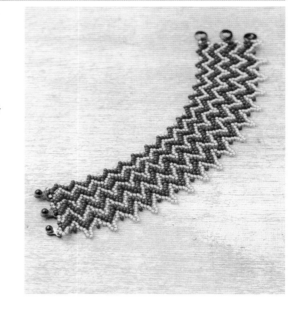

What you will need:

- 8g x size 11° seed beads in each of A & B

- 3 x snap clasps (to tone with the beadwork)

Foundation Row:

1 With a good, long wingspan, using A for the main colour and spacers, and B for the body beads, work a foundation row in Basic HorSO WH (don't forget to add a spacer bead between every stitch of the bracelet) to span your wrist, allowing 1cm/½˝ gap for the clasps.

2nd Row:

2 Work the 2nd row in Basic HorSO WH (B – main colour and spacers; A – body beads).

3rd Row:

3 Work the 3rd row in Basic HorSO WH (A – main colour and spacers; B – body beads).

4th Row – Transition (Basic to 2-Drop):

4 The upright stitches are 2-Drop HorSO WH and the inverted stitches are Basic HorSO WH (B – main colour and spacers; A – body beads).

5th Row:

(5) Work the 5th row in 2-Drop (A – main colour and spacers; B – body beads).

6th Row:

(6) Work the 6th row in 2-Drop (B – main colour and spacers; A – body beads).

7th Row:

(7) Repeat row 5.

8th Row – Transition (2-Drop – 3-Drop):

(8) The upright stitches are 3-Drop and the inverted stitches are 2-Drop (B – main colour and spacers; A – body beads).

(9) Weave around to secure the final stitch and use the working thread to attach the clasps, then finish off.

(10) Finish off the tail thread.

(11) Work in a new thread to attach the remaining clasp halves.

Variations

- This lovely curved beadwork could easily be extended into a collar, and you needn't stop at 8 rows. The graduation works best with 3 repeat rows in one stitch, then a transition row, then 3 repeat rows in the next size larger stitch, and so on. Attaching only one small snap clasp at the foundation row would allow the beadwork to settle nicely over the shoulders without puckering.

- I think it would be fun to use drop or dagger beads for the head beads in the final row, which would make it lovely and spiky!

- Don't just stick to 2 colours, choose graduated tones – say from dark to light, run through the rainbow or go random. As I mentioned before, that will need a little planning because for every row you will need to pick up body beads for the inverted stitches that will be the main colour of the next row.

The gorgeous stone drops I've incorporated into these earrings, provide a perfect sloping face on which to display transitioning waves, and it's great fun selecting the colours to complement the stones. Strongly contrasting colours or finishes really accentuate the growing waves. We're taking another step forward in Hubble skills with this design as you are working Basic, Transition and 2-Drop WH in tubular and HorSO mode. However, once mastered, these pretty beaded bead caps take very little time to work, as there are only 6 stitches in each row. I couldn't resist making a pair in each of the stones I had. (See page 79.)

What you will need:

- 0.5g x size 15° seed beads in each of A & B

- 32 x size 15° Czech Charlotte seed beads or Czech seed beads (to match A)(C)

- 12 x size 15° Czech Charlotte seed beads or Czech seed beads (to match B)(D)

- 2 x size 11° seed beads (to match A)(E)

- 2 x daisy spacer beads (to match A)(F)

- 2 x teardrop stone beads 30x8mm, fully drilled (faceted or unfaceted)(G)

- 1 x pair ear wires

1st Row:

1 With 1m/40" thread, pick up 6A. Pass through all 6 again to form a ring, and once more through the first A bead picked up.

2nd Row:

2 Place 1A between each of the 6A of the ring, and step up into the first A bead of this row.

3rd Row:

 Work a row of Basic HorSO WH using A for the main colour, B for the body beads and C for the spacers.

Don't forget to pick up that final spacer bead before joining the 6th stitch onto the 1st. Remember you'll have to do this on every row!

Close the row and secure it (see Notes on page 5). Snuggle up.

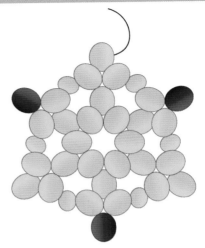

4th Row:

④ Transition (Basic to 2-Drop): The upright stitches are 2-Drop and the inverted stitches are Basic (B – main colour; A – body beads; D – spacers). 1st stitch: 4B+1B; *2nd stitch: 1D,2B,1A; 3rd stitch: 1D, 4B+1B*. Repeat from *to* once, then repeat the 2nd stitch once more and pick up 1D. Close the row and secure.

Heads up! There are no C or D beads in these 3 final rows as we're fanning out wider, so we'll be using A and B beads as spacers because they're larger. So, for each of the 2nd – 6th stitches, remember that the 1st A or B bead picked will be the spacer bead and is not part of the stitch.

5th Row:

⑤ Work the 5th row entirely in 2-Drop (A – main colour and spacers; B – body beads). 1st stitch: 4A+1A; *2nd stitch: 5A,1B; 3rd stitch: 5A+1A*. Repeat from *to* once and the 2nd stitch once more. Pick up 1A, close the row and secure.

6th Row:

⑥ Transition (2-Drop to 3-Drop): The upright stitches are 3-Drop and the inverted stitches are 2-Drop (B – main colour and spacers; A – body beads). 1st stitch: 6B+1B; *2nd stitch: 5B,1A; 3rd stitch: 7B+1B*. Repeat from *to* once and the 2nd stitch once more. Pick up 1B, close the row and secure.

7th Row:

7 Work the 7th row entirely in 3-Drop (A – main colour and spacers; B – body beads). 1st stitch: 6A+1A; *2nd stitch: 7A,1B; 3rd stitch: 7A+1A*. Repeat from *to* once and the 2nd stitch once more. Pick up 1A, close the row and secure.

8 That completes the beaded bead cap, so finish off both the working and tail threads. Now let's assemble the earring.

9 With a new 40cm/16" thread:

a) Pick up 1F and 1G.

b) Pass through the centre of the beaded bead cap (from the wide end to the narrow end).

c) Pick up 1E and pass back through the bead cap, G and F.

d) Pick up 1C and pass back through the F, G, bead cap and E.

e) Pick up 9C and pass through E in the same direction as before, making a ring.

f) Pass again through the 9C and E.

g) Pass through bead cap, G, and F.

h) Tie together the working and tail threads, snuggling up all components. Don't cut the threads.

i) Pass through C, and tie the threads together again.

j) Pass through all components to emerge from the E bead; cut the working thread.

k) With the tail thread, pass through C, then through F, G and bead cap, and cut off.

10 Add the ear wire and that's one earring completed. Now make it's partner!

Variations

- The teardrop stone in the black and gold earrings below is heat-treated agate, and it's also faceted so it catches the light as it turns. To give a little extra sparkle, I added a 2mm faceted black spinel bead below each daisy spacer.

- Make a picot with the Charlotte beads at the base of the teardrop by picking up 3C instead of 1.

- For a bigger bead cap statement, substitute a fringe dangle or drop bead for the head bead of each of the 3-Drop Hubbles.

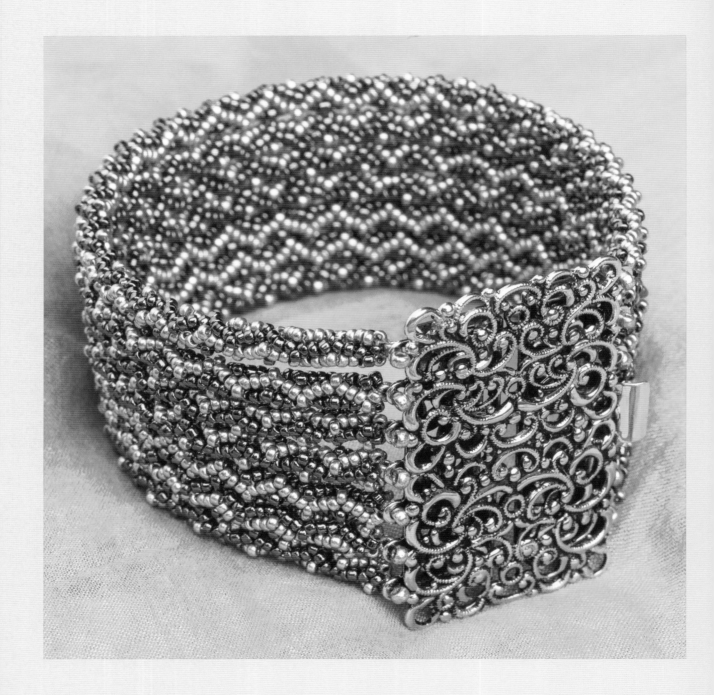

CHAPTER SIX

· · ·

Horizontal Wave Hubble Ropes

CHAPTER SIX

Horizontal Wave Hubble Ropes

I could hardly wait to write this chapter since the second I hit upon the WH rope. I've been itching to share this technique, as I think this has to be one of the most exciting and fun things you can do with WH and one of the most interesting ropes to incorporate into your designs.

Both normal Hubble and WH can be used to create wonderful ropes in a number of different ways. We can apply the same principles to these ropes as we have done with Hubble cuffs, that is, not only can they be worked vertically, but also horizontally. In this chapter we'll focus on the Horizontal WH rope version and later look at incorporating the HorSO technique.

Just to be clear about this whole horizontal/vertical thing: vertical ropes are made as tubes that grow in length with the addition of each new row, whereas the horizontal WH rope is made lengthwise, in other words, the foundation row you cast on is the entire required length of the rope. You then work two more rows and the real fun bit comes when you zip the 4th row onto the 1st. I always find zipping up peyote stitch tubes rather satisfying and enjoyable; if you feel the same, then you'll absolutely love this.

The only drawback with setting the length of the rope from the first row onwards, is that you may need to change the length at a later stage. So it's important to understand that you can't reduce the length of the rope once it's made, but the good news is that you can easily add to it seamlessly. So, make sure you are certain about the required length or, if not, reduce it slightly so you can add to it.

Once you've worked 3 rows, you simply fold the 1st and the 3rd towards each other to work the zip-up 4th row; you'll see that the rows hinge beautifully from one to the next, so the rope in cross-section is actually a tiny square. It has a lovely feel to it and is very, very slinky. Sorry to go on, but I just love it!

I advise working a small swatch of, say 11 stitches; I'm suggesting you work an odd number, so you can start each new row with an upright one. Once you are au fait with the technique, you can work even numbers (if you've worked the Kelim Earrings then you'll be fine starting the row with an inverted stitch), but I want you to be able to focus on one thing at a time, so you can really have fun with this.

I also advise working in 2 contrasting colours of size 11s to begin with, so you can see the dynamics of this technique and maintain a good tension throughout.

Foundation Row:

With 1m/40" thread, A for the main colour and B for the body beads work a foundation row of 9 stitches. Step up.

2nd Row:

Work the 2nd row with B for the main colour and A for the body beads, and step up.

3rd Row:

Work the 3rd row with A for the main colour and B for the body beads, and step up.

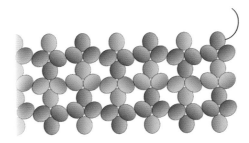

Heads up! It's zip-up time, so to prepare the beadwork, gently fold the 1st and 3rd rows around to face each other. See what I mean about the way they hinge nicely along the length of the rows? It's a useful property. The diagram below shows what the resulting folded beadwork should look like. I've made the 2nd row pale to indicate that it lies in the background, and you can clearly see the body beads form an alternating pattern across from each other. I've slightly exaggerated the appearance of the holes in the arm beads below the body beads, but in reality you won't see those holes as clearly, because the stitches should be very much more snuggled up – so it's just to make a point and distinguish between the inverted and upright stitches. The most important thing to understand now is that for this zip-up row, **every** presenting body bead will become a head bead, so you won't need to pick up any new head beads as they're already in situ, waiting for you. Let's have a go!

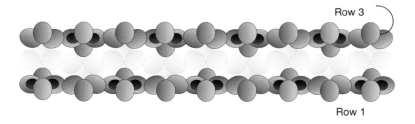

4th Row:

You will only be picking up B beads for this row.

1st stitch – **Phase 1**: With the thread emerging from the end head bead of Row 3, pick up 2B and pass once more through that head bead.

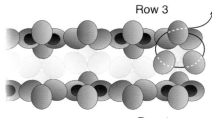

Phase 1 (cont.): Pass through the 1st B picked up in the same direction – this positions the 2 arm beads.

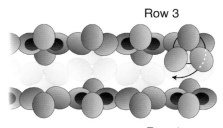

Phase 2: Pass through the awaiting body bead opposite on the Row 1 side of the beadwork (so it becomes your new head bead), then through the 2nd arm bead to complete the stitch. Snuggle up.

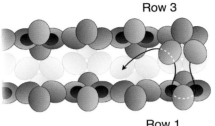

Row 3

Row 1

2nd stitch – **Phase 1**: Pick up 2B, backstitch through the head bead on the Row 1 side; pass through the 1st B picked up in the same direction. Snuggle up.

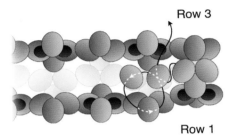

Row 3

Row 1

Phase 2: Pass through the awaiting body bead opposite on Row 3, and on through the 2nd arm bead to complete the stitch. Snuggle up.

The 3rd stitch will be built on the Row 3 side, picking up the head bead from the Row 1 side, and vice versa for the 4th stitch. Continue zipping up in this way until the row is finished and the rope completed. Keep snuggling all the way!

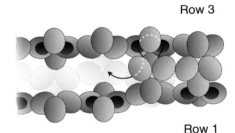

Row 3

Row 1

Finishing off a WH rope

Take a look at one end of the rope; there are 4 prominent arm beads (one from each of the 4 rows) and a thread will be emerging from one of them. To neaten the rope end, use that thread to run around all 4 arm beads and pull them together; now you can either finish off the thread by weaving back down into the Hubbles, or sew on a finding of your choice. Do the same at the other end.

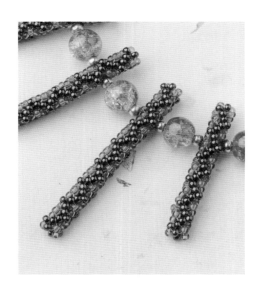

Wave Rope Variations and Inspirations

Erika Simons had a great idea and made this fun, jazzy necklace with a variety of short lengths of 4-way (4 rows) Basic WH rope, using size 11s, and interspersed them with pretty crackle beads on Tigertail. She kept them all in place with crimps.

Don't forget that you can work horizontal ropes in good old, normal Hubble stitch - they are really pretty and lacy.

As you have seen, working the Basic WH rope in 4-way makes it quite fine (gorgeous in size 15s), but you can make a thicker, 5-way version in the same way, just by adding one row and using the 5th row as the zip-up. The drawback is that you can't use 2 contrasting colours, as 5 is not an even number, however you can make it all in 1 colour or 5 different ones. If you use 5 different colours, make sure that you think ahead when working the foundation row because the colour of the body beads of the **upright stitches** must be the colour of the zip-up row. So if you set out your colours A, B, C, D and E, and begin your foundation row, the pick-up sequence for the first two stitches, which are repeated along the length, will be: 1st stitch: 2A,1E+1A; 2nd stitch: 2A,1B+1A. In this way you have set up the body beads on the upright Hubbles, which will be ready to be the head beads for the 5th row when zipped together.

You'll see that the larger you go with the stitches the more of a latticed structure the rope becomes. Experiment with 5-way or 6-way, 3-drop versions and the core size of the rope will be quite large, to the point where you could insert a string of small crystals or pearls along the length for some inner sparkle or lustre. Erika Simons created the gorgeous 5-way, 3-Drop WH rope necklace (page 6) – it's so serpentine and slinky!

HorSO WH ropes are the bees knees! You may remember, back in Chapter 5, I mentioned how helpful it is to employ the HorSO technique when making ropes, because they grow more quickly and remain just as beautiful. For an elegant 4-way Basic HorSO WH rope your spacer beads must be the same colour as the main colour you are using for the row. The pick-up sequence for the first 2 stitches would be: 1st stitch: 2A,1B+1A; 2nd stitch: 3A,1B+1A (then ignore the 1st A picked up). Then simply repeat the 2nd stitch until you have the required length of foundation row. Take care when working the zip-up row as it's easy to forget to pick up the spacer beads between the stitches. The Basic HorSO WH bracelet shown on page 80, was made using size 15s. I'd had that spectacular clasp in my stash for a long time and had planned to make something wildly elaborate with it, but one day I spotted it amongst my findings and realised I didn't want to detract from its beauty, so I simply attached a number of ropes to show it off rather than swamp it.

I experimented with 2-Drop WH ropes and found the softest, and most beautiful by far, was the 5-way HorSO one – it has an interesting springy or spongy nature and holds its shape perfectly. The 4-way 2-Drop one is more rigid and textured because the head beads tend to sit a little more prominently from the rest, but the 4-way has its place and would be useful as a slightly less flexible structural tube/rope. For the 2-Drop 5-way HorSO version you will need to think ahead exactly the same way as for the 5-way Basic one, that is,

incorporating the 5th colour for the body beads of the upright stitches in the foundation row. The pick-up sequence for the first 3 stitches is: 1st stitch: 4A,1E+1A; 2nd stitch: 5A,1B+1A, 3rd stitch: 5A,1E+1A. The 2nd and 3rd stitches are then repeated until you reach the desired length (work an odd number of stitches for the foundation row until you are really comfortable with this technique). The 5-way, 2-Drop HorSO WH rope bracelet (above) was made by Erika Simons (she really loved making these ropes) and she's incorporated 2 pretty bead caps at the ends with a magnetic clasp - very effective! If you don't want to fiddle around with clasps, work the 5-way, 2-Drop in circular mode and create a bangle; these roll on and off your

hand very easily. The two bangles on the previous page are examples of 2-Drop and 2-Drop HorSO – can you work out which is which?

If you're feeling particularly enthusiastic, try making a 4-way Basic HorSO WH rope entirely in Charlottes. I made the Venezia necklace rope using 24kt gold-plated, size 15° Czech Charlottes (yes, crazy lady, I know, but I can be forgiven at least, for using the HorSO technique). Interestingly, due to the shaping of Czech Charlottes, the rope had a more rounded feel to it, as opposed to a more square cross-section.

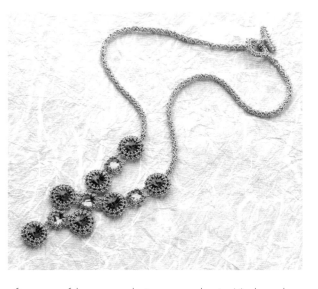

And now a little something for the guys. For years I wanted to bead something for my son but could never settle on anything that would be appropriately masculine for him, until he popped in to see me one day whilst I was making a sample of the normal, 4-way Basic HorSO rope in a single colour of size 15s. I showed him what I was doing and instantly he asked me to make him this rope for one of his carved stone pendants. He loved the feel and precision of the beadwork, then he asked what colours I had (I know, what a fun question to ask a beader); as he was wearing an earthy coloured top, I picked out some #2035 beads (one of my faves – I worked some of the mountains in them on the Atlantic View Bracelet), and he said 'That's the one!' I made it and he's never taken it off.

CHAPTER SEVEN

· · ·

Toroids and Toggles

Toroids and Toggles

When I began writing this book I had great difficulty teasing out the order of the chapters and deciding which project should go where, but gradually logic prevailed, although it didn't help that the more I wrote, the more I discovered. Then I had to decide if I could fit it all in and, guess what, I couldn't! So, fellow Hubbling fiends, be warned there is still more yet to come.

In this chapter it'll feel like I've scooped up all the techniques you've learnt throughout the book, and thrown them into one big melting pot! It's challenging, but it wouldn't be a decent final chapter if you didn't get to surround at least one cabochon, and you get the chance to do just that in Project 8.

When I got the Hubble gang together for our second WH session, I showed them 4-way WH ropes. Whilst everyone was still getting to grips with WH, there was understandably a little loose tension going on, but that caused one of those serendipity moments. One rope was so soft and flexible that it could be curled into a loop. I realised I just had to try and properly engineer an entire standalone ring or toroid (shaped almost exactly like a POLO® mint or Life Savers®, because in section it is a square). It was dead simple to do, with a bit of help from the HorSO technique for the 2nd, 3rd and 4th (zip-up) rows.

The foundation row is the innermost surface, which then allows easier zipping up at the end. I shall elucidate as you try it out. You will need (surprise, surprise) 2 contrasting colours of size 11° seed beads (A – dark and B – light), and 1 colour of size 15° seed beads (C) to match B exactly.

Foundation Row:

1 This is the innermost and, therefore, the shortest surface of the toroid, and the stitches will be orientated to face each other (much like that fairground ride where everyone stands in a ring with their backs to the wall inside a huge rotating 'drum', holding hands and whizzing round very fast). You'll need an even number of stitches so that the inverted last stitch can be joined to the upright first stitch. We'll start with a 10 stitch toroid, so cast on 10 Basic WH stitches using 2A,1B+1A as the pick-up sequence for each stitch. Join the last stitch onto the 1st to form the ring (close the row) and secure it as normal, emerging from the head bead. Don't worry about trying to make all the stitches behave right now, because they'll be corrected as you work the 2nd Row.

Workshop Tip 9: I've not mentioned snuggling up for a while, as I hope, by now, you're really good at snuggling, but I must emphasise here, that it's a really important part of the technique in order to achieve a lovely, solid toroid.

2nd Row:

2 This row makes the equivalent to one of the surfaces on the mints where you would see the printed words. It also has a greater distance to cover than the foundation row. To achieve this we'll work a HorSO row using C beads as the spacers between each stitch. The spacers blend into the waves as they are the same colour as the B beads, and the entire row forms a pretty, 5-point star pattern (it's worth noting that the number of points in the pattern always corresponds to half the number of stitches worked in the row). The pick-up sequence is as follows: 1st stitch: 2B+1B; *2nd stitch: 1C,2B,1A; 3rd stitch: 1C,2B+1B*. Repeat from *to* three more times, then repeat the 2nd stitch once more. Don't forget that all important final spacer bead, C, as you close the row and secure it.

3rd Row:

3 The outermost edge of the toroid covers the greatest distance, and we achieve this by working another HorSO row, but this time using the A beads as the spacers between the stitches as they are size 11 and push the stitches further apart, whilst blending in with the waves. The pick-up sequence will be: 1st stitch: 2A+1A; *2nd stitch: 3A,1B; 3rd stitch: 3A+1A*. Repeat from *to* three more times then repeat the 2nd stitch once more. Again, don't forget the final A spacer when closing the row.

Workshop Tip 10: Your beadwork most likely looks more like a tube than the beginnings of a toroid. If you remember when you were working the linear rope, you could fold the rows as if they were hinged. The same applies here, only it's just a tad fiddly - the 1st and 3rd rows must be folded towards each other awaiting the zipping up. This image may help to give you some perspective on the folded structure which is like a little gutter; the pale green body beads situated alternately on rows 1 and 3 are clearly displayed, and you can see Row 2 at the bottom of the gutter shape.

4th Row (Zip up):

4 Now we're making the final face of the toroid which is essentially the same as Row 2, inasmuch as it will look identical when completed. It's a zip up row, as the head beads are already in place, and we're back to using the C beads as spacers again. So the pick-up sequence will be: 1st stitch: 2B; 2nd stitch: 1C, 2B. Repeat 2nd stitch eight more times. Final spacer bead reminder (sorry to harp on, but it's so easy to forget), now close the row and finish off.

Variations

• Here's where the toggle idea comes in, because a toroid is quite a sturdy, little structure, excellent for use as a toggle ring. By working a short length of linear WH rope to span the diameter of the toroid, you have the perfect matching toggle bar. Have a go at making one in the final project – Sand Dollars.

• Once you've practised with a 5-point (10 stitch) toroid, try making larger ones by making 2-stitch increments to the foundation row, simultaneously adding 1 point to the wave pattern. The toroidal elements of the necklace and bracelet shown on page 90, are 6-point toroids, worked in size 11° seed beads around 16mm vintage, jonquil rivolis. The rope element is a vertical, 4-stitch, WH tube.

• Embellish the inner spaces or outer surfaces of the toroids to make interesting pendants, earrings or bracelet components - there are plenty of attachment points.

• Don't stop at Basic WH toroids, try working them in 2-Drop or 3-Drop WH. The 2-Drop, 6-point toroid in pink and grey (page 105), has surprisingly smooth and rounded surfaces, not squared off like the Basic one (technically making it a Torus, to all you beady mathematicians out there, as it's more circular in section), and the whole structure is extremely solid.

• String an eclectic collection of toroids in different sizes, stitches and colours onto a rope (of any kind).

• For a grand statement, make a chain of toroids, building each new one onto the last.

Here we are at the final project and, as before, I've drawn together almost all the WH techniques you've met in this book, plus a little more. We're going to have some fun setting rivolis inside our toroids. When I made the first rivoli element, I loved the way the five body beads lying prominently against each rivoli face appeared to be almost floating unattached. Adding a delicate latticework on the front really brought out the star pattern, and I was immediately reminded of pretty Sand Dollars in the sea, that I'd picked up when swimming in Florida, hence the name. There are at least ten points of attachment on these elements, so they can be used in necklaces and earrings too. For this bracelet I used Picasso Green and Duracoat Galvanised Gold seed beads and Hyacinth rivolis.

Bracelet length: 18cm/7½". If you need to lengthen the bracelet, each rivoli unit and connector adds 2cm/3/4".

What you will need:

- 7 x 14mm Swarovski rivolis
- 7g x size 11° Miyuki seed beads (A) (Picasso Green)
- 5g x size 11° Miyuki seed beads (B) (Gold)
- 2g x size 15° Miyuki seed beads (C) (Gold)

Toggle Ring

We'll start with the toggle ring because the rivoli units are worked along the same lines. Work a 5-point toroid exactly as directed on pages 93-94. Finish off the working and tail threads.

Rivoli Unit

These units are essentially the same as the 5-point toroid toggle you've made, except that Row 1 is omitted to allow the rivoli to fit inside. So the structure comprises the 2nd, 3rd and 4th rows of the toroid, with no zipping up, and we'll start with the 2nd row as the foundation row (please don't hate me!).

Foundation Row:

1 1st stitch: 2B,1A+1B; 2nd stitch: 1C,2B,1A+1B. Repeat the 2nd stitch 8 more times and, remembering to add the final spacer bead, close the row and secure.

2nd Row:

2 Work as for the 3rd row of the toggle ring (using A for the main and spacers, and B for the body beads).

3rd Row:

3 Work as for the 2nd row of the toggle ring (B – main, A – body and C – spacers) but, just before closing the row, slip the rivoli inside. Secure and weave on to emerge from a head bead at the rivoli face, as in the diagram.

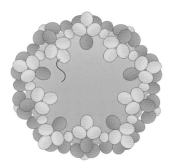

Heads up! You've probably noticed that the little structure is not a particularly tight fit, so we will now add a decorative row over the face of the rivoli, which will also secure it. This row is modified brick stitch, which I call 'Up&Along'. You'll soon see why.

4 With the thread emerging from the left side of the head bead, pick up 5C; backstitch through the next head bead along on the right (this means pass through it from right to left) and pass back through the last 2C picked up, in the opposite direction.

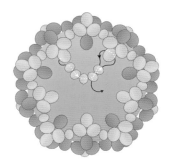

5 Snuggle up the beads so no thread shows between them.

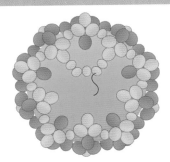

6 Pick up 3C, backstitch through the next head bead and pass back up through the last 2C picked up, in the opposite direction. Snuggle up.

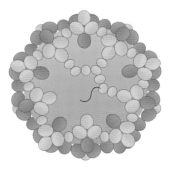

Workshop Tip 11: I find this 'Up&Along' technique incredibly useful for bezelling cabochons, because by modifying the number of either the 'Up' or the 'Along' beads you can tailor the beadwork to the cabochon. In this design the 'Up' beads are the two beads that are shared between two stitches, and the 'Along' beads are the single, unshared ones, so the pattern is 2Up&1Along.

7 Repeat step 6 two more times, snuggling all the time.

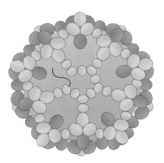

(8) All that remains is to fill in the last 'Along' bead as the 'Up' beads are already there in the 1st stitch of this row. Pick up 1C and pass down through the first 2C of this row towards the head bead; backstitch through the head bead and pass back up the same 2C in the opposite direction. Snuggle up.

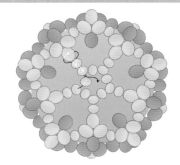

(9) Weave through the thread path of the 1st stitch in this row to the next head bead and finish off in the beads at the back of the rivoli.

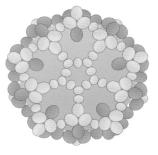

Toggle Bar and Chain Links

(1) For the bar, simply cast on a foundation row of 5 Basic WH stitches with the following pick-up sequence: 2A,1B+1A.

2nd Row:

(2) *1st stitch: 2B+1B; 2nd stitch: 2B,1A.* Repeat from *to* once, and the 1st stitch once more.

3rd Row:

(3) *1st stitch: 2A+1A; 2nd stitch: 2A,1B.* Repeat from *to* once more and repeat the 1st stitch again.

4th Row:

(4) Zip up with B beads only.

(5) Turn the beadwork to look at the end of the short section of rope; you can see 4 arm beads there. With the thread emerging from one of the arms of an end Hubble stitch, pass around all 4 end stitches and pull together tightly. Weave along to the opposite end and repeat.

6 Now for the attachment loop: Weave back to a central B head bead of the 2nd or 4th rows and pick up 9C. Pass through the head bead again making a loop.

7 Pass around all the loop beads once more, snuggling them up; weave back into the bar and finish off.

8 **Chain Links**: With 20cm/8" thread, pick up 11C and pass through the loop of the toggle bar. Pass through the 11C again and the toggle bar and the 1st C picked up again. The 11C are now a chain link that needs to be secured. *Make a half hitch knot and pass through the next 2C*. Make sure the link is snuggled up and there is no visible thread. Repeat from *to* several times, pass through 4C and cut off. Repeat the procedure for the tail thread, which will be woven in the opposite direction, thereby really making the little link secure.

9 Following the procedure in step 8, build a 2nd chain link from the 1st. Set this component aside for now.

Double Hubble Connector and Connecting the Rivoli and Toggle units

Although these little rivoli and toggle units have no bilateral symmetry we won't have a problem connecting them. First we need to make a tiny Double Hubble connector!

1 Make one Hubble thus: 2B,1A+1B.

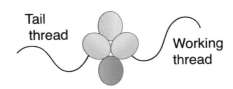

Tail thread

Working thread

2 Pass the needle through the body bead to emerge as in the diagram.

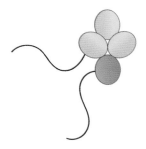

3 Make a 2nd Hubble on the same body bead thus: Pick up 2B, pass through the body bead and the 1st arm bead picked up, then pick up 1B for the head bead and pass through the 2nd arm bead.

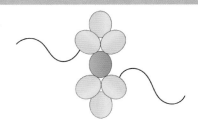

4 a) Bring 2 rivoli units together, placing them back to back, and hold them so you are looking at the edges.

b) Rotate the units until the waves on the edges match up, pointing in the same direction.

c) Place the Double Hubble connector between the units at the head bead of one wave and the body bead of the other.

d) With the working thread emerging from the arm bead of the 2nd Hubble, pass the needle through the head bead at the tip of the right hand rivoli unit wave.

e) Continue on, passing through the arm, head and arm beads of the 1st Hubble to emerge on the left side (where the tail thread is emerging, but not shown in this diagram).

f) Pass through the body bead of the wave tip on the left hand rivoli unit.

g) Continue on through the arm, head and arm beads of the 2nd Hubble.

h) Snuggle up.

i) Pass around the entire circuit again, weave into the right hand rivoli unit and finish off.

j) With the tail thread, weave around the circuit and finish off.

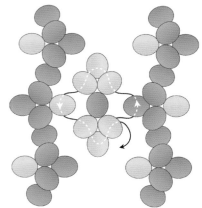

Left rivoli unit edge - Row 2   Right rivoli unit edge - Row 2

Connect all the units in this way, including the toggle ring. Use one bead of the final chain link on the toggle bar as if it was the body bead of another rivoli unit, and connect the final rivoli unit in the same way.

Variations

- These rivoli units are connected together in a straight line for the bracelet, but they could be connected in a curve for a necklace.

- By working the 'Up&Along' on the reverse side of the rivoli units you can display the full crystal face and stabilise the unit from behind, as in the Jonquil necklace and bracelet shown on page 90. Bear in mind that for different sized rivolis and toroids, you will have to tailor the beadwork by modifying the numbers of the 'Up&Along' beads.

- By using size 15° Czech Charlotte seed beads or Czech seed beads rather than the larger size 15° Miyuki seed beads for the 'Up&Along' row, you can achieve more delicate lines across the face of the cabochon. Again, you will need to modify the numbers for each stitch to tailor the beadwork to the cabochon.

Hubbling to infinity and beyond!

Our journey to this point has taken us into some fantastic realms on planet Hubble. All of the techniques in this book can be embellished, exploited and manipulated to the max, as well as mixed in with other beadwork stitches, to produce stunning beadwork. There is still so much more to explore, and the more I play with this stitch, the more I discover.

In the Sand Dollars project you've already had a little taste of Double Hubble, a simple technique from which I've developed a sparkling science called Chatonology; join me in book three and you'll meet it on the next stage of our quest.

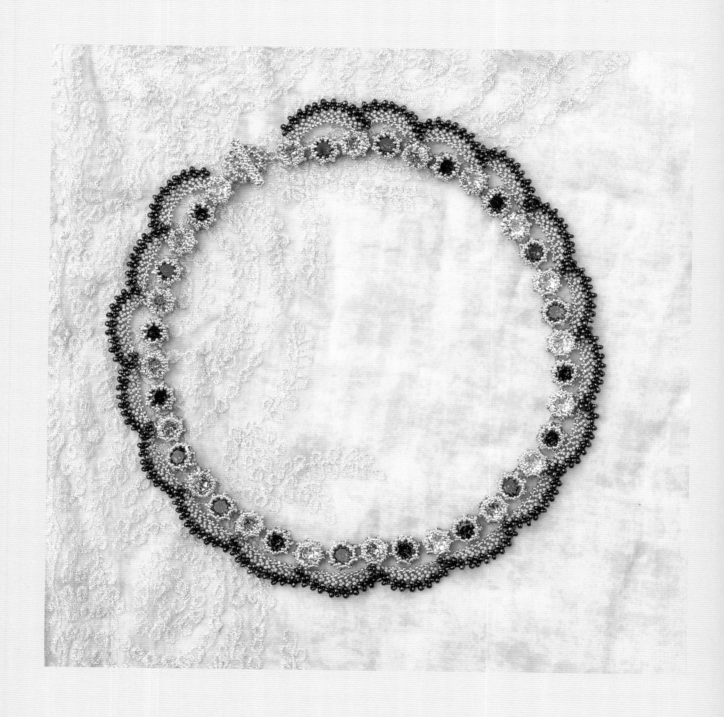

THANKS AND ACKNOWLEDGEMENTS

THANKS AND ACKNOWLEDGEMENTS

I now find myself in a different position from when I was writing my thanks and acknowledgements for *Let's Hubble!*, because at that point I had no idea how Hubble stitch was going to fare in the beading world. On the day of my book launch at the Great British Bead Show Sunday bazaar in May, 2015, which was actually the day before its official launch, I will never forget my friend and publisher, Sue's face when she walked over to my table. Sue looked at me, dead pan, and asked if I wanted the good news or the bad news. I went cold, thinking I had missed a typo or an incorrect diagram in the editing, but not wanting to tease me any more, she grabbed my arm and said she'd already sold out of her stock and needed mine! I was floored – I just couldn't believe it and was enormously buoyed up by the news. It was one of the most exciting days in my life because I also won a prize in the Swarovski Crystal Anniversary competition with a necklace made entirely in Hubble stitch – and I'd never entered a beading competition before either!

Book sales continued really well to the point that we quickly went for a second print run, and I began teaching Hubble stitch all around the UK, and subsequently in the US. I can only describe myself as absolutely overjoyed with the way Hubble stitch has been embraced by the beading world. I started getting emails from beadworkers who had tried it and loved it, so I made a specific Hubble stitch Facebook page where they have been sharing their work to help inspire others, and, not least of all, designers and tutors have been incorporating Hubble stitch into their beady creations.

All of this spurred me on to get cracking with book two, because I just had to share Wave Hubble with everyone. I had a much more clearly defined understanding of exactly what was required of me to put together a book and I set about it with gusto. I gathered my little Hubble gang together – somewhat reduced due to various grandchildren commitments, and the Wave Hubbling started in earnest, whilst I began to write. Huge thanks go to Nitty Chamcheon, Erika Fidler and Erika Simons for their patience and hard work, learning Wave Hubble and producing fab pieces for this book; we had so much fun at our get-togethers sorting out everything from beadwork to politics, fuelled by good old, home-cooked nosh and cake.

Almost a year, to the day, after that Sunday at the Great British Bead Show, I clicked send, and all the *Hubble Stitch 2* files whooshed over to my publishers. I felt a real rush of excitement and anticipation for what was in store for Wave Hubble. I knew book two would be in expert hands when I sent it, as they had made my first publishing experience such a joy; I owe Sue, Kelly, Mark and Maria enormous gratitude for their help, support and professionalism.

My thanks must also go to Michael Wicks who, once again, provided the beautiful images for this book; his photographic expertise speaks for itself.

Writing thanks and acknowledgements really takes me to a place of deep introspection, especially when thinking about the role of my family. Steve is my rock and my best friend, bringing me a cuppa and a kiss when I'm having a moan about some diagrams, and not complaining when I come to bed at 3am, because I can't sleep without finishing the next chapter. To me those little things mean total love and support. My children, James, Gemma and Louise, have their own busy lives to lead, but always have time to comment on my latest design, and I know I've made them very proud when I hear them telling friends, 'My mum's written a book!' I have a wonderful ambassador for my beadwork and books in my mother; she wears my beadwork when going shopping and walking her dog, enthusiastically directing everyone who asks about the jewellery to my website. So I give my greatest thanks to my wonderful family for their love and unquestioning encouragement.

Contact details

Email: beadschool@gmail.com
Website: www.beadschool.co.uk
Facebook: Melanie de Miguel (Beadschool Mel)
YouTube: Beadschool – Melanie de Miguel
Twitter: @BeadschoolMel